FALLING OFF THE PODIUM

PODIUM

and Other Life Lessons

Phenomenal Publishing Inc.

ISBN 978-0-9802448-47

To order additional copies, please contact us at:

www.PhenomenalPublishing.com

FALLING OFF THE PODIUM

and Other Life Lessons

John V. Sinclair

*This book is dedicated
to Gail: my wife and best friend.*

The love of my life!

Table of Contents

INTRODUCTION

MORE OFTEN THAN NOT, the life and work of a conductor are an impenetrably mysterious business to non-musicians. Exactly what is he doing waving that stick around up there on the podium—and who taught him how to wave it?

Conductors don't play anything, and yet they conjure up music out of thin air, and everyone, including their colleagues, watches them do it. In my experience, no line of artistic work is harder for laymen to understand. Yet conductors, perhaps in part because of this seemingly inexplicable aspect of their careers, tend to be fascinating creatures, and on the rare occasions when they write memoirs, the results are always worth reading.

I've known John Sinclair for the better part of both our lives and have worked closely with him in a wide variety of capacities, always with pleasure and profit. Not only is he a superbly accomplished artist, but he's also a great storyteller; the kind of man with whom you always look forward to dining after a performance. Yet I'd only heard a handful of the tales that he tells in *Falling Off the Podium ... and Other Life Lessons*, some of which are charming and funny, others deeply poignant, and all immensely interesting to read.

John is, like me, a small-town boy from Missouri, a regular guy (something that can't be said of all that many conductors!) who ended up making his way in the larger world of art as a musician, teacher, and conductor. I started out as a musician and knew some of the people about whom he writes in these pages, and every word he writes, about them and everything else, has the bright ring of remembered, fully told truth.

As John says in "You Can't Hide", one of the concise, pithy essays that make up *Falling Off the Podium*, "Music exposes phonies." It sure does, and so does writing a memoir. To read this one is to come away certain that its genial author is one of the least phony musicians—and men—you could ever hope to meet.

What strikes me most forcibly about John's book, however, is the accumulated wisdom that is to be found in between his stories. He is a thoughtful artist, and a humane one. It is precisely because there is so much more to him than music that there is so much more to his conducting than mere baton-waggling. Knowing him has been one of the signal pleasures of my life, and you'll get to know him as he really is in the pages of this book. Needless to say, that isn't true of all memoirs, but reading *Falling Off the Podium* is…well, almost as much fun as having dinner with its author after a concert. I can't say better than that!

—Terry Teachout

TERRY TEACHOUT is the drama critic of the Wall Street Journal and the author of biographies of Louis Armstrong, George Balanchine, Duke Ellington, and H.L. Mencken. He has also written two plays, Satchmo at the Waldorf *and* Billy and Me, *the libretti for three operas by Paul Moravec, and the text for Moravec's* Music, Awake!, *a choral work premiered in 2016 by John Sinclair and the Bach Festival Society of Winter Park.*

Chapter 1

Common Sense 101

"Horse sense is the thing a horse has which keeps it from betting on people."

—*W.C. Fields (1880-1946)*

My grandfather was a bit of a Will Rogers type who always had something folksy yet profound to say — although usually minus the humor.

When I earned my undergraduate degree from William Jewell College, he gave me two presents. One was a silver dollar minted the year he was born, 1902. The other was a little card that read, "No college ever gave a degree in common sense!"

It was a simple version of Victor Hugo's saying, "Common sense is in spite of, not the result of, education."

During a visit to my grandfather's store after a long week of teaching, he asked if I had made anybody mad. I replied that I didn't think so. "Are you sure you showed up at work?" he asked. "You can't teach without challenging someone."

As a child, to earn my candy allowance, my chores at the store were seasonal. In the winter, I carried coal for the potbelly stove. In the summer, I was required to grow a vegetable garden because my grandfather believed that "everyone should know how to grow their own food."

Often, I'd clean the century-old wooden plank floors by sprinkling sawdust on them and then sweeping it up. If I ever sought praise for my competence, my grandfather's answer was always the same: "Don't expect a compliment for just doing your job."

Perhaps the paramount lesson that I learned from my grandfather was of the value of a strong work ethic. I was surrounded by a whole family who never missed work and never stayed home, even when they probably should have.

I'm not sure if that's a strength or a weakness, but I'm a subscriber to Shakespeare's contention that "There is plenty of time to sleep in the grave."

Over the past 20 years, I've conducted over 800 Candlelight Processionals, 300 Bach Festival programs, and hundreds of other concerts. And while my grandfather would be indifferent to my being a conductor, he'd respect me for having never canceled, called in sick, or made an excuse.

I feel a bit like Ella Fitzgerald when she said, "They say even iron wears out. I think if I ever just had to sit down, I'd say to myself, 'What am I going to do now?' "

Woody Allen once noted that "about 90 percent of success is showing up." It's trite, but does make an important point. The most difficult part of accomplishing any task is getting started — and showing up is the first step.

Now, don't think I can't procrastinate, because in 1973 I purchased a book entitled *Do It Now: How to Stop Procrastinating*. As you might have guessed, I haven't read it yet.

"I was obliged to work hard. Whoever is equally industrious will succeed just as well."
　　　　　—J. S. Bach (1685-1750)

Cracker Jacks

"I have a dream that one day little black boys and girls will be holding hands with little white boys and girls."
—*Martin Luther King, Jr. (1929-1968)*

I spent the first 11 years of my life in a small town of 200 people before my family moved to Independence, Missouri, a suburb of Kansas City. In that little town, my grandfather's store sat directly across from the Santa Fe and Wabash train tracks.

Like most little boys, I was fascinated by trains. At the age of 8, I convinced my family to take me to Kansas City and put me on a train so I could ride it — unaccompanied — to a nearby station. No good parent would permit such an adventure today, of course, but this was 1962 — a very different time — and in the Midwest. It was a thrilling, 45-minute trip. The train even had a diner car.

When I reached my destination, I was carrying five boxes of Cracker Jacks. My mom asked about all the boxes, and I told her that I had bought them from a porter in the diner car. I had been so fascinated by this man that I had gone to the diner car five times, and bought a box every time.

My mom asked, "What was so special about this man?"

The answer? The porter was black, and I had never seen a black man up close. I asked him if I could see his hands. He obligingly held them out and rotated his palms up. I touched them, and said, "You're just like me."

I've never forgotten his response. "Son," he said, "I'm like you in every way, and maybe one day everyone will see that." This took place during the turmoil of the civil rights movement. I met a kind, gentle soul who recognized innocence — and took the risk of teaching a young boy a lesson about life.

Rarely does this sort of transformative education take place in a classroom. Ray Charles thought that he could "let you know all about the heartbreak, struggle, lies, and kicks in the ass I've gotten over the years for being black … without actually saying a word about it."

It's reflections like this that make me especially proud to be a musician. A few years ago, one of our college administrators asked me how our department of music has recruited so many minority students.

My response was simple. We don't care how someone looks, what they believe, or who they love, I told him. All we want to know is, "Do you love music, are you a good person, and how well do you play or sing?"

Jazz guitarist Bill Frisell once said, "For me the music community was always like a model for what could be. The way people would play together, just harmony and being — old guys and young guys, black guys and white guys."

"I'm trying to get people to see that we are our brother's keeper, I still work on it. Red, white, black, brown, yellow, rich, poor, we all have the blues."

—B.B. King (1925-2015)

Big Shoulders and Tough Roots

"For a tree to become tall it must grow tough roots among the rocks."

—*Friedrich Nietzsche (1844-1900)*

We all stand on the big shoulders of those who have come before us. Often, they're the shoulders of our teachers. I've been very fortunate to have studied with magnificent teachers; too many to mention here, but appreciated always.

Music majors study music theory. It wasn't my favorite, but it was necessary. One day, my undergraduate theory professor, Mr. Edward Lakin — whom students had nicknamed "The Scorekeeper" — asked me to stop by his office after class.

Mr. Lakin often addressed us very formally, so when I arrived at his office he said, "Mr. Sinclair, you got a B on your last assignment." I responded, "Yes sir. Is there a problem?"

He repeated himself, but with more intensity. "Mr. Sinclair, you got a B on your last assignment." I uncomfortably replied, "But that's a pretty good grade." Mr. Lakin agreed that a B wasn't a bad grade — but stated that it wasn't an acceptable grade for me.

He then asked why I hadn't done better. I explained that I had a gig with my band the past weekend, and didn't have much time to work on my theory. Mr. Lakin said that he and I needed to have an understanding: If I didn't do my best work in his class, I would be repeating it the following year.

I was a musician with a future, he said, and I would need a

good theory background. I left his office rather stunned, and frankly a bit angry. But guess what? I never came to his class again without having done my best work — and I never had to take additional theory for my master's or doctoral degrees.

Mr. Lakin had indeed read me correctly. I had considered theoretical studies to be a necessary evil instead of the gateway to musical insight.

I now use my comprehensive theory education every day of my professional life, and I'm so indebted to Mr. Lakin for his unorthodox, yet extremely effective, manner of motivation.

I had a number of interactions with Mr. Lakin over the years. What I found, as you might suspect, was that he had a servant's kind heart, but a tough core. Martin Luther King, Jr. said it best: "We must combine the toughness of the serpent with the softness of the dove, a tough mind and a tender heart."

Thank goodness Mr. Lakin was my theory professor.

"Education is helping the child realize his potentialities."
—Erich Fromm (1900-1980)

As You Practice

"Practice does not make perfect. Only perfect practice makes perfect."
—*Vince Lombardi (1913-1970)*

As a musician, the discipline of daily practice and study is engrained in my very being. Like most professional musicians, I feel a bit guilty if I don't pursue my craft each day.

During a rehearsal in my early years of teaching I blurted out, "As you practice, so shall you perform." It seems that I've recited this statement — and lived by it — incessantly for my entire career.

In 1976, my students gave me a plaque inscribed with that admonition, which they had heard me repeat so many times. And 40 years later, my current students have inscribed the same words on a sign hanging in front of our rehearsal hall.

I've found meaning and inspiration in the often-quoted saying of Aristotle: "We are what we repeatedly do. Excellence, then, is not an act, but a habit."

In his book *Outliers*, Malcolm Gladwell writes, "The idea that excellence at performing a complex task requires a critical minimum level of practice surfaces again and again in studies of expertise. In fact, researchers have settled on what they believe is the magic number of true expertise: 10,000 hours."

Undoubtedly, 10,000 hours may, to some, seem an arbitrary number. But whatever the right number is, there's no question that achieving expertise requires a huge investment of time. Innate talent certainly helps, but talent alone doesn't allow you to skip mandatory hours of dedication to your art.

The martial artist Bruce Lee put it this way: "I fear not the man who has practiced 10,000 kicks, but I do fear the man who has practiced one kick 10,000 times."

There seems to be a belief that prodigies may ignore this commitment. Most academicians would agree that the world has never seen a more natural and productive musician than Mozart, but Mozart himself wrote, "It is a mistake to think that the practice of my art has become easy to me. I assure you, dear friend, no one has given so much care to the study of composition as I. There is scarcely a famous master in music whose works I have not frequently and diligently studied."

Two centuries later, Irving Berlin summed it up even more succinctly when he said, "Talent is only a starting point."

I've known hundreds of musicians with great natural talent who lack the discipline to persevere. What also transfers with experience is consistency. And to paraphrase Aristotle, this is where excellence becomes a habit.

What makes sense to me is this quip: "Hard work beats talent when talent doesn't work hard."

Being a true night owl, I rarely going to bed on the same day I get up. Patrick Rothfuss, in his book *The Name of the Wind*, helped me put this habit in perspective when he wrote, "Music is a proud, temperamental mistress. Give her the time and attention she deserves, and she is yours. Slight her and there will come a day when you call and she will not answer."

So I began sleeping less to give her the time she needed.

In summary, if musicians are able to practice like they perform, then they shouldn't have performance anxiety. After all, they're only practicing.

"If I miss one day of practice, I notice it. If I miss two days, the critics notice it. If I miss three days, the audience notices it."

—*Ignacy Jan Paderewski (1860-1941)*

Lots of Luck, the Last Sub ...

"Be who God meant you to be and you will set the world on fire."

—*St. Catherine of Siena (1347-1380)*

I student-taught at Harry Truman High School in Independence, Missouri, during the first semester of my senior year in college. At the time, I was making my living and paying my way through college teaching trumpet lessons — 30 students a week — directing a church choir, and playing gigs.

I was hoping to have a full-time teaching position in the fall, so I decided to substitute teach in the interim. As it turned out, I received a subbing assignment that lasted six weeks, through the end of the school year.

A variety of unusual events happened during my first week. The choral program to which I was assigned had gone through at least nine substitutes (subs) since the choral director had left a number of months earlier.

To say that the students had taken over the classroom was an understatement. The administration let me know it would be difficult, and to call if I needed help. They also said that there were some students with behavioral issues in my classes.

When I arrived on my first day, I was told that in my classroom many of the doorknobs were loose, and that the bottom rungs of many of the chairs were broken — so be careful.

The vice-principal walked me to the choral room. I was greeted with a banner made of construction paper draped over the piano. It read, "Lots of luck, the last Sub...."

St. Catherine of Alexandria, the patron saint for teachers, must have been watching out for me. Rather than just babysit the class for the rest of the year, I thought we should try to make music.

I was inside my office, auditioning a few students, when I looked out my window into the rehearsal room and saw a disturbance. I quickly ran out to investigate.

When I grabbed the doorknob, it came off in my hands. When I moved a chair that was in the way, the legs bent. Everyone sat down and got very quiet, very quickly.

On my second day, we started singing. An eighth-grade student continued talking as we tried to rehearse. "Jimmy, please sit down and quit talking," I said. His response was immediate and completely unexpected.

He charged me with something in his hand. I dodged him and pinned him on the ground, frantically shouting for a student to call on the intercom and ask for some help from the principal's office.

The principal arrived within a minute and escorted Jimmy out. The next day, I found out that he had been institutionalized — and in his hand, when he charged me, was a small knife.

What else could go wrong? Actually, the Friday of my first week was the most difficult to handle. I noticed a seventh-grade girl named Becky crying, and I asked her what was wrong.

The story she told was heart wrenching. Through her sobbing, she said that her mother's new boyfriend had choked her younger brother until he was unconscious when he resisted going to bed. I immediately told the story to a vice-principal, who in turn contacted family services.

Becky was moved to a foster home in another area. I never saw her again, but have often wondered what happened to her.

That night, I talked to my fiancée about my eventful week. What should have frightened me away left me more certain than ever that teaching was a noble calling — and that I was made for the profession. I finished the semester and was indeed "the last Sub."

Henry Adams said that a teacher "affects eternity; he can never tell where his influence stops." Being a fourth-generation teacher, teaching was the family business — and I can honestly say that I've never regretted choosing this profession.

"Teaching is a 24-hour, seven-day-a-week job because when you invest in kids, you never stop caring."

—Anonymous

Compliments are Poison

"Humility is not thinking less of yourself, but thinking of yourself less."

—*C.S. Lewis (1898-1963)*

Take your work and purpose seriously, but not yourself. I've discovered that a person who loves himself or herself more than anyone else won't have any competition.

Early in my teaching career, an elderly man approached me and introduced himself as having a similar last name, "St. Clair." He said, "I've been seeing your name in the paper lately, so can an old man give a young man some advice? I was an ambitious, hot shot, young attorney. Now, as an old judge, let me share this insight."

Then it came: "Compliments are like poison. If you touch some to your tongue and spit it out, you'll live, but when you swallow it and believe it, you'll die."

As difficult as it might be for some of us to accept compliments, I've learned that receiving them is also an art — and to not do so graciously could be perceived as an insult to those offering praise.

I've never been especially good at offering idle praise. My good colleague, Edmund LeRoy, once suggested that if you weren't impressed with a particular presentation, you could use lines such as, "quite remarkable", "amazing program", or, perhaps most inscrutable, "that was really something."

I was once told that if you praise everyone, then you praise no one. As Will Rogers reminded us, "Get someone else to blow your horn and the sound will travel twice as far."

And have a purpose. J.S. Bach didn't disguise his aim. He signed many of his works with the initials "SDG," which stood for Soli Deo Gloria, or Solely for the Glory of God.

> *"Humility is the Mother of giants. One sees great things from the valley and only small things from the peak."*
> —*C.K. Chesterton (1874-1936)*

Mesmerized by Marilyn (Horne)

*"You have to know exactly what you want out of your career.
If you want to be a star, you don't bother with other things."*
—*Marilyn Horne (b. 1934)*

When you get right down to the basics, music is an aural art form, and we musicians learn our craft by listening. We listen to our teachers, to one another and, perhaps most importantly, we listen critically to ourselves.

My alma mater. William Jewell College, has a performing arts series second to none, and like most college students, I didn't realize its impact at the time. With hindsight, I now know that this great series informed my entire career.

To hear performers of international acclaim, at the top of their respective games, raise the bar extremely high allowed me to truly recognize excellence.

In four short years, I heard such artists as Luciano Pavarotti, Beverly Sills, Jessye Norman, Isaac Stern, Andres Segovia, Vladimir Ashkenazy, James McCracken, Leontyne Price, and dozens of other legends, including the incomparable mezzo-soprano Marilyn Horne.

I was allowed to be the page-turner for a recital featuring Ms. Horne. Her singing was magnificent, beautifully warm and rich. I had never been so close to such an instrument. During the concert, I remember being mesmerized by that glorious voice. And then I heard her famous accompanist Martin Katz say, "Turn the page."

I snapped out of my trance and turned the page. Then I heard him say, "Again." I had simply gotten lost in the sound, and was embarrassed. Luckily for me, no one was the wiser, because Mr. Katz had memorized her recital.

Fast-forward nearly 30 years. Ms. Horne came to Winter Park to perform a gala concert to commemorate the successful end of a Rollins College capital campaign, and we were accompanying her with a combination of college and Bach Festival musical forces, which I conducted.

After the rehearsal, I shared with Ms. Horne the story of turning pages at her recital during my college years. She laughed so hard that tears well up in her eyes, as she recalled that she and "Marty" had shared a good laugh at my expense.

The next day, as we took a curtain call at the end of our concert, Ms. Horne gave me a hug and whispered in my ear, "I'm so proud of you, John — you didn't get lost tonight."

The lighthearted goading about my brief and ignoble stint working with one of the great singers of the 20th century — and Ms. Horne's back-handed compliment — is an experience that I'll always cherish.

"In order to be a great composer, one needs an enormous amount of knowledge, which ... one does not only acquire from listening to other's people's work, but even more from listening to one's own."
—*Frederic Chopin (1810-1849)*

Do They Pay You for That?

"The best work never was and never will be done for money."
—John Ruskin (1819-1900)

My grandfather was a gruff guy who wore dark gray work clothes, and almost always had a stubbly beard. He also had an artificial eye due to an accident as a child. Mothers tell their children not to run with sticks. Well, my grandfather was the little boy they were warning us about.

He owned and operated a general store in Camden, Missouri, a small town an hour from Kansas City. This was the only job he ever had. The store had been in the family since the 1840s, and he remembered working there when he was 5 years old in 1907.

You could usually find him in his store or in his garden — but concerts, formal gatherings, or even churches were not in his wheelhouse.

Still, my grandfather was very bright and always had music in his home. My mother was a pianist, and my grandmother was always singing. By all accounts his mother — my great-grandmother — was cultured and sophisticated.

But as close as my grandfather got to a concert was watching The Ed Sullivan Show on Sunday nights. Or, if my grandmother had her way, The Lawrence Welk Show.

During my first year of teaching junior high school, I took my grandfather to a concert I had organized and was conducting. For the occasion, he wore his one and only suit, and his good wide-brimmed hat.

The concert, which featured four of my choirs, was held in the school's cafetorium, a multi-purpose room that doubled as a lunchroom and an auditorium. Not exactly a classy concert venue.

Afterward, I asked my grandfather what he thought of the concert. You could tell he was developing his answer when he hesitated, and then asked, "Do you get paid for that?" I responded that this was, indeed, my job.

"You're having too much fun to get paid," he quickly replied.

That has become my mantra. It seems to me that if you're not enjoying yourself when making music, then you might be in the wrong profession. To make music for a living — to have a profession that doesn't feel like you're going to work — is a privilege. I always tell my students that making music is as much fun as you can have legally.

When an audience can see that you're enjoying yourself, the audience has permission to do the same. Comedian Red Skelton once said, "If we're having fun, the audience is having fun."

"I've never known a musician who regretted being one. Whatever deceptions life may have in store for you, music itself is not going to let you down."

—Virgil Thomson (1896-1989)

I Hear the Rolling Thunder

"And I heard a sound from Heaven like the roar of mighty ocean waves or the rolling of loud thunder."
—*Psalm 77:19*

As a college student, one of my part-time jobs was singing for a large funeral home. I always got tickled when the funeral home called and asked for "live" music. Families were allowed to select from a long list of offerings, and they often chose the hymn "How Great Thou Art."

I showed up at the appointed time for the funeral, and the organist, with whom I had never worked, greeted me. She was a thin, elderly lady wearing a red-and-white polka-dot beret, which she wore sideways.

We exchanged pleasantries. She asked if we needed to practice, and neither of us thought it was necessary.

The time for the solo arrived, and I began to sing from behind a curtain, "O Lord my God, When I in awesome wonder, consider all the worlds Thy Hands have made; I see the stars, I hear the rolling thunder."

As soon as I sang "rolling thunder," the organist played a loud two-handed glissando, trying to imitate thunder by sliding her fingers up and down the scales. The theatrics of the imitation thunder greatly amused me, and I barely got through the song. My throat had closed and tears were streaming down my face as the service thankfully came to an end.

Immediately afterward, the funeral director walked directly up to me. I was thinking, "Oh no, a perfectly good job lost." He looked quite serious when he told me, "The family wanted to express how much they appreciated the fact that you were so touched."

One's perception becomes one's own reality and truth. The philosopher Friedrich Nietzsche said, "All things are subject to interpretation. Whichever interpretation prevails at a given time is a function of power and not truth."

"Be grateful for luck and pay the thunder no mind."
—Eubie Blake (1887-1983)

Chapter 2

Ebony and Ivory

"There are two ways of spreading light — to be the candle or the mirror that reflects it."
—*Edith Wharton (1862-1913)*

During my four years teaching at East Texas Baptist University, I saw much of the country through a tour-bus window. Like choirs at many denominational schools, ours served an ambassadorial role and often went on the road to perform.

On a Houston-area jaunt, we scheduled a concert at a high school north of the city. We followed our normal pre-concert routine, and the presentation was typical in every way — until I announced an encore.

I introduced the tune by reciting the words of the song and commenting that they were "words to live by." Some of my students looked tense as we sang Paul McCartney's "Ebony and Ivory." I hadn't seen those looks before.

As soon as we completed the song and the concert, several of my students approached me and suggested that we not linger. Even a few of the men in the choir walked with me, and encouraged me go straight to the bus.

As we pulled away from the school, I asked why we needed to be in such a hurry. Little did I know that we had just performed "Ebony and Ivory" in a town known for its large KKK faction.

This same town made the national news as late as 1998 for the brutal murder of an African-American man by three white supremacists.

During my second year at Rollins College, I went to a suburb of Orlando to work with a high school choir. As I drove by the town hall, three men were holding a rally, walking in a circle holding signs. They were KKK members, complete with white robes.

I pulled over, got out of my car and watched in disbelief. The image was surreal. How could this public display of contemptible ignorance and hate exist?

My patriotism understands and defends every American's right to assemble. But my idealism can't rationalize allowing openly racist and discriminatory behavior.

This should be beyond the pale of public decency, and it's a crime. It is not an entitlement. Certainly, this is not what was envisioned by our Founding Fathers. The fact that long ago, Socrates said, "There is only one good — knowledge; and one evil — ignorance," informs us that this is not a new topic.

Woefully, the lyrics to "Ebony and Ivory" are as relevant today as when they were when they were written, more than 30 years ago. Albert Einstein lamented that, "What a sad era when it is easier to smash an atom than a prejudice."

Would it not be the most notable of accomplishments if, during our era, we confronted and defeated all types of bigotry? If we're truly ever to become a United States of America, it is incumbent upon every citizen to condemn intolerance.

Ebony and ivory live together in perfect harmony
Side by side on my piano keyboard, oh Lord, why don't we?
We all know that people are the same where ever you go
There is good and bad in ev'ryone
We learn to live, we learn to give
Each other what we need to survive together alive.

—Paul McCartney (b. 1942)

Hey, Look Me Over

"Look at me, and be astonished. And put your hand over your mouth."

—Job 21:5

Timing is everything, not only in music but also in life. Years ago, while I was teaching high school, I got a call from the local funeral home asking if I was responsible for the band practicing on the field across the street from their establishment.

I responded that as department chair, I supposed that I was responsible. The funeral director said that a visitation was taking place, and that the band could be heard. I apologized, but explained that there was only one practice field, and only one time available for rehearsal.

The funeral director said that they were accustomed to hearing practices. The problem this time, he explained, was the song being played: "We just opened the casket up for viewing and the band started playing "Hey, Look Me Over."

Choosing the right time to say or write something can be an art form. The Internet may be the most important invention since the printing press, but I'm convinced that we create plenty of problems by pushing the Send button too quickly. As you know, we used to write or type our letters and think them through before anyone read our thoughts.

A few years ago, in the Rollins College library, I saw a student who had just sent me an email. I approached her and answered her question, after which she looked quite surprised and said, "I thought you'd just email me back."

With the convenience that the Internet and todays social media afford also comes responsibility. We can never forget that what's being communicated online is one keystroke away from being public information.

I'm concerned about another important aspect. Because of the extensive use of the Internet, we could be losing the art of conversation — and even more frightening, losing a genuine investment in one another.

"My friend told me there was life outside the Internet and that I should check it out, so I asked him to send me a link."

—Anonymous

Fried Macaroni

"Tradition is not the worship of ashes, but the preservation of fire."

—Gustav Mahler (1860-1911)

Most musicians have habits or rituals — I prefer to call them "traditions" — that we observe prior to a performance.

I don't have the proverbial lucky cufflinks — though I do have a favorite pair — or a token in my pocket. But while I'm onstage, a couple of ibuprofen, a glucose tablet, and a handkerchief are never far away.

I will always conduct my first concert during the annual Bach Festival while I'm wearing a new pair of socks. And prior to that first performance, I'll eat a very specific meal: fried macaroni and a grilled-cheese sandwich.

I'm often asked about the recipe for fried macaroni. It's easy: boil it, drain it and, like any good unhealthy food, fry it in lots of butter. Over the years, however, dietary demands have changed my eating habits. The macaroni is now whole wheat, and the grilled-cheese bread is multigrain. But it still accomplishes the same thing.

The tradition goes back to when my wife Gail and I were dating. I would stop by her parents' home after an evening of teaching trumpet lessons, and she would often cook this meal for me. So, it's comfort food — and something we share.

This ritual helps to ground me, and put my work in perspective. It reminds me that my work would simply not be possible without my wife Gail, my willing muse.

Mark Twain said: "To get full value of joy you must have someone to divide it with."

And Hector Berlioz combined the power of music and love when he said, "Love can give no idea of Music, but Music can give an idea of Love. ...Why separate the two? They are the two wings of the soul."

In my case, they're intimately entwined.

"There is no place for grief in a house which serves the Muse."

—Sappho (c. 630-c. 570 B.C.)

Musical Protein

"If music be the food of love, play on."
—William Shakespeare (1564-1616)

We all have our favorite junk food — and sadly, I'm an overachiever in this area. I am firmly convinced that when I finally meet up with St. Peter at the Pearly Gates, he will have orange fingers and orange crumbs on his robe from the unlimited supply of Cheetos and Butterfingers in Heaven.

Just like us, many great composers were "foodies." Beethoven loved trout and eggs (often raw), and was fastidious with his coffee, insisting on 60 grains per cup.

Brahms was also particular in brewing his own extremely strong coffee, with lots of cream. His favorite dining establishment was called the Hedgehog Inn.

Liszt often ate bacon and eggs, and partook of libations when composing. Rossini and Grieg were gourmands. Rossini was as prolific as a chef as he was as a composer. And Grieg was known to love oysters, and would linger at delicatessens.

Handel was a big man and a heavy eater. And Mendelssohn, who also had a hearty appetite, celebrated food culture while traveling. He wrote about food in his letters, and had an affinity for German sausages and English butter pudding.

Like any good German, Bach loved his wine, beer, and coffee. There's a coffee stain ring on an opening page of his Mass in B Minor. And his Coffee Cantata tells of the disputes in mid-18th century Leipzig surrounding the drinking of coffee. It's great fun to humanize these composers by discussing their diets.

Does the food we eat correlate to our musical listening habits? I think it was one of my professors, Dr. Eph Ehly, whom I first heard use this analogy. Here's my take on the comparisons.

Many people go through life sustaining themselves on "Twinkies" of music. Much of the music we listen to has no nutritional value. It's void of intellectual or spiritual purpose. It goes down easily, is entertaining, and fills a void — but it's wasted carbs.

Functional, durable music is equivalent to good carbs. This class of music is equivalent to vegetables, fruits, and whole grains. Solidly written music is important for good health.

When you need protein to sustain you, however, then you turn to the masters. Brilliant compositions by master composers feed your body, mind, and soul. Timeless masterpieces are works that will speak to you, and encourage you to grow each time you hear them. This kind of nutrition is life changing.

Enjoy desserts and good carbs, but don't deprive yourself of cerebral and spiritual musical protein.

How is your musical diet?

"Cannibals don't eat clowns because they taste funny."
—Anonymous

Give 'Em Hell

"I never did give them hell. I just told the truth, and they thought it was hell."
—Harry Truman (1884-1972)

Growing up in Independence, Missouri, you're not only allowed to quote Harry Truman, it's a requirement. For a history buff like me, having a former U.S. President living in my town provided plenty of opportunities.

President Truman left the White House and truly became a private citizen. Therefore, many residents of Independence have their own Truman sightings.

He and Bess lived a block away from the junior high school I attended. I have a fond memory of the president stopping by our band room to hear "Hail to the Chief" during one of his morning walks.

Lieutenant Westwood of the Independence Police Department accompanied President Truman on his walks. This was before Secret Service agents protected past presidents.

You could sometimes even see the president's silhouette through the window of his home, as he sat in a chair, reading.

Often, dignitaries and other politicians came to visit Independence's most famous resident. I saw, among others, Hubert Humphrey, President Johnson, Richard Nixon, and Robert Kennedy make their way to President Truman's house.

A few years ago, author and historian David McCullough spoke at Rollins College at the Winter Park Institute. After his appearance, I drove him to his hotel and asked if he was hungry. He responded, "I'm hungry and I need something to drink."

So what was supposed to be a brief stop ended up being a long meal, during which Mr. McCullough shared his impressions of the time he spent in Independence while researching his Pulitzer Prize-winning biography on President Truman.

I told him that my mother wrote the President every year to ask for an autographed picture, which she would give to the highest-achieving student in her sixth-grade classroom. Truman would always respond, writing, "How nice it is to hear from you again, Mrs. Sinclair."

My mother-in-law tells the story of a friend going grocery shopping with a young child. President Truman, who was waiting in his Chrysler for a staff member, volunteered to babysit while the family was in the store. He said he was pleased to do so because he missed his grandchildren.

President Truman was a wonderful gentleman. My final memory associated with him is of playing Taps at a local ceremony commemorating his life.

Harry Truman faithfully did his damnedest.

"He held to the old guidelines: work hard, do your best, speak the truth, assume no airs, trust in God, have no fear."
—David McCullough (b. 1933), in Truman

Bach To the Future

"Bach opens a vista to the universe. After experiencing him, people feel there is meaning to life after all."
—Helmut Walcha (1907-1991)

When I was an undergraduate, I remember saying to my mom, "Oh no, don't remind me — I have to attend that classical guitar recital tomorrow." I really wasn't sure what to expect, but I dreaded sitting through a long solo concert. Little did I know that the experience would change my life.

Not knowing what I didn't know, I was unimpressed that the guitarist happened to be none other than Christopher Parkening. And what happened that evening was transformative.

At the time, I was studying classical music — but I was really much more interested in jazz and rock. That evening, I learned two major things: First, I completely understood why Bach is so important. Second, I realized that in the hands of a true artist, the music of Bach —who, after all, wrote for virtuosos — is truly perfection.

The first piece on Mr. Parkening's program was an enthralling Bach Prelude and Fugue. The virtuosity he displayed gave the music clarity and fluency. It was like hearing it for the first time.

That evening, I became a Bach devotee. And I've been trying to explain his expansive genius to the world ever since.

Mr. Parkening had come to my alma mater, William Jewell College, to play a guitar recital, not to teach. But an artist teaches every time he or she plays. As Stephen King writes, "We never know which lives we influence, or when, or why."

A few years back, the Bach Festival Society presented Christopher Parkening during our Visiting Artists series. I shared with him how much he had influenced me. I told him that when I heard him play, years before, I had fallen in love with the music of Bach — and for that, I was forever grateful.

In Mr. Parkening's typical humble response, he thanked me for relaying the story and for allowing him to influence me. I responded, "Don't you have that backwards?" But as I considered Mr. Parkening's words, I began to ask myself this: Isn't this as good as it gets?

We all hope our passion influences others, who will in turn inspire others still. This is the principle reason we teach.

"Bach is the supreme genius of music ... This man, who knows everything and feels everything, cannot write one note, however unimportant it may appear, which is anything but transcendent. He has reached the heart of every noble thought, and has done it."
—Pablo Casals (1876-1973)

Hallelujah!

"His hallelujahs open the heavens. He utters the word 'Wonderful,' as if all their trumpets spoke together. And then, when he comes to earth, to make love amidst nymphs and shepherds (for the beauties of all religions found room within his breast), his strains drop milk and honey, and his love is the youthfulness of the Golden Age."
—*Leigh Hunt (1784-1859)*

The Hallelujah Chorus from George Frederic Handel's Messiah is perhaps the most recognizable and majestic chorus of western culture.

I have a sordid past — or at least a love/hate relationship — with this great work. It isn't from lack of experience, because I couldn't begin to count the number of times I have conducted it. Surely, it's in the thousands.

Even though I sang the Hallelujah Chorus once in college, my first in-depth exposure to the work was while teaching high school. The tradition of the school where I worked was to invite choir alums to stage to join in its singing.

So, to be respectful, at our Christmas concert I kept the tradition alive. I asked, "In keeping with tradition, would our alumni please join us for the singing of the Hallelujah Chorus?" I'm not sure what I expected, but it certainly wasn't the mob that came forward.

The singing was rather innocuous until the end of the piece, where everyone cuts off. Then there's a grand pause before the last four notes are sung.

A few sopranos whose vibrato was big enough to drive a

44

truck through — and not touch either side — didn't seem to want the pause, or to cut off.

They held last note for what seemed like an eternity. I remember trying to cut if off three times before the horrific sound stopped. The piece is pitched a bit high anyway, and very few soprano sections make it sound attractive. (Handel never heard it that high because Baroque-era pitch was lower.)

I approached the Hallelujah a bit differently my remaining years at the school. The conductor who started that tradition was still living in town, so out of the kindness of my heart — and the protection of my psyche — I asked her to conduct. Everyone loved it — especially me.

The audience standing during the singing of the Hallelujah Chorus is a tradition with murky origins. Some sources believe that at the Messiah's London premiere in 1743, King George II was so moved that he stood in reverence. Yet others believe that he was tired of being seated — after all, it is Movement 44 out of 53.

A few cynics believe the King stood because of a medical condition, making it uncomfortable to sit for long periods. The answer could be any or none of these explanations. A number of musicologists question whether or not the King was even present.

How did the tradition of standing make it "over the pond?" It's believed that Benjamin Franklin, who attended a performance in Dublin in 1759, might have been the first to stand in America.

Thanks a lot, Mr. Franklin!

"Vibrato — controlled is an ornament; uncontrolled, a disease."
—Attributed to Arturo Toscanini (1867-1957)

Beauty and Beyond

"O my Luve's like a red, red rose
That's newly sprung in June;
O my Luve's like the melodie
That's sweetly play'd in tune."
—*Robert Burns (1759-1796)*

After my love for my wife, my children, and music, comes my love for roses. I only grow fragrant Tea varieties, but it isn't just the fragrance. It's the rose's elegance, form, and beauty that I hold in reverence.

All humans have an organic and innate need to have beauty in their lives. This has been the case throughout the ages. It was validated to me during a trip to Turkey, where we saw ancient Roman ruins. Even early Christian cave dwellers had artwork on the walls and ceiling.

We also know that all early civilizations had music.

There's a Persian proverb that says, "He who wants the rose must respect the thorn." It's a wonderful lesson that anything so beautiful must be treated with care. This comparison is apropos when I'm preparing to conduct a musical masterpiece.

I visualize myself holding a priceless artifact, and being careful not to stumble while carrying it. My job is to make sure that such beautiful art makes it safely to the ears of the audience.

Nearly 40 years ago, we bought a charcoal drawing of a beautifully graceful ballet dancer. When we inquired about the artist, we discovered that he was a prisoner who had been incarcerated for life. How could the same person who had created this elegant, refined art have murdered someone?

A letter from the inmate accompanied the drawing. I keep the letter, and each time I read it I become even more confused. He wrote, "It's just the joy that it can bring to an individual that is more then (sic) will to share the joy of making something ..." and he signed it, "Love, Peace, and Happiness."

This led me to question what might have happened if this person had enjoyed the benefit of education, or had been surrounded by more beauty in his life.

I'm aware that what I contribute to this world is considered fluff to some. But, I find peace and validation in the fact that my work attempts to produce beauty — and that the need for art is an answer, not an option.

Let's hope that Fyodor Dostoyevsky was correct in believing that "Beauty will save the world." And St. Augustine, who said, "Beauty is indeed a good gift of God." And Kahlil Gibran, who said, "Beauty is eternity gazing at itself in the mirror."

The German writer and philosopher Johann Wolfgang von Goethe wrote, "To keep young, every day read a poem, hear a choice piece of music, view a fine painting and, if possible, do a good action. Man's highest merit always is, as much as possible, to rule external circumstances, and, as little as possible, to let himself be ruled by them."

I encourage each of you to embrace great art, and to make sure you experience it every day. It will feed you intellectually, emotionally, and spiritually.

Meanwhile, don't forget to heed these popular song lyrics: "You got to stop and smell the roses; you've got to count your many blessings every day."

"Beauty of whatever kind, in its supreme development, invariably excites the sensitive soul to tears."
—Edgar Allan Poe (1809-1849)

Chapter 3

I'd Wake Up Rufus

"Nothing behind me, everything ahead of me, as is ever so on the road."

—*Jack Kerouac (1922-1969)*

When confronted with a sudden problem, I like to remember this story:

Roy was interviewing for a truck driver's job, and the interviewer presented him with this scenario: "Roy, you're driving an 18-wheeler high in the mountains and starting down a steep grade, the road is iced over, your brakes have failed, and there's no pulloff road. What are you going to do?"

Roy thought a moment and said, "I guess I'd have to wake up my driving buddy, Rufus." Why, the interviewer asked, would you wake up Rufus? Roy replied, "'Cause Rufus aren't ever seen a wreck like we're gone have."

When conducting, you must often think fast on your feet. Many times, I've wanted to "wake up Rufus." But when a mistake happens, I've learned to visualize putting the problem in a jar. I say to myself that I'll revisit the issue when I've had time to think about it.

I've found that when you dwell on the past — and especially your mistakes — it clouds your vision of the present and the future. Author Phyllis Theroux says, "Mistakes are the usual bridge between inexperience and wisdom."

Believe me, there'll be plenty of time later to beat yourself up — and when you do, open the jar with care.

As Will Rogers said, "Don't let yesterday use up too much of today."

Or, better yet, as Nelson Mandela stated, "The greatest glory in living, lies not in never failing, but in rising every time we fall."

I believe in the famous saying, "Too much ego will kill your talent."

"You must have the score in your head, not your head in the score."

—Hans von Bulow (1830-1894)

You're Still Too Loud

"We're working with dynamics now... We've learned after the last two years, that what's really important is that the music be groovy, and if it's groovy enough and it's well-played enough, it doesn't have to be loud."
—Jerry Garcia (1942-1995)

Nearly 30 years ago, when I was chorus master for an opera company, the conductor summoned me to the orchestra pit, in the middle of a scene, and asked if I could hear the choir.

I replied that I couldn't. He asked why not. I replied, "Well, the choir is way back on the stage and the tenor up in front is really loud." The conductor asked me to stay where I was while he resumed the rehearsal.

He promptly stopped the orchestra and again asked, "John, can you hear the choir?" I said again that I couldn't. He asked why not, and I hesitated to reply because I knew that I was being set up.

Finally, I repeated, "The choir is way back on the stage." The conductor then asked, "Is there anything else?" I replied, "The tenor is really loud."

The tenor soloist promptly lifted his chin arrogantly, glared at me and said, "Too loud? You know, young man, I am from the New York Metropolitan Opera." I responded, "Sir, I have never even been there, but you're still too loud."

He stormed off the stage, and refused to return unless I apologized. The general manger told me that I needed to apologize. I felt I didn't say anything wrong, so I refused to do so.

While I was sitting on the hot seat, I remember hearing the orchestra shuffle their feet to express approval of my remarks — and I noticed broad smiles on the faces of the choir.

The Bible says, "Then you will know the truth, and the truth will set you free." (John 8:32) On that occasion, I found out that while the truth might set you free, it might also get you in trouble.

So what to learn from this? Again, the Bible offers insight: "For by your words you will be justified, and by your words you will be condemned." (Matthew 12:37)

Choose your words carefully. I could have been more kind and diplomatic. Words have power and consequences, and can be hurtful. Frankly, I thought the tenor deserved it. But his bad behavior didn't warrant mine. Eating your words is like eating bad leftovers.

I might also add that we need to be especially careful when dealing with the ones we love. Hurtful words to our loved ones have a direct line to the heart and soul, and can be even more damaging.

Maya Angelou wrote, "If you have only one smile in you, give it to the people you love. Don't be surly at home, then go out in the street and start grinning."

"When in doubt, sing loud."
—Robert Merrill (1917-2004)

Losing Your Ass in the Bargain

President Lincoln often quoted the 15th-century poet John Lydgate, who wrote, "You can please some of the people all of the time, and all of the people some of the time, but you can't please all of the people all of the time."

That saying should be the Conductor's Creed.

When confronted with the type of disagreements that require a decision bound to please one individual more than another, I invite the litigants into my office, and start by telling this story:

A man and his son are on their way to market with a donkey carrying a heavy load of produce to sell. Not too far into the journey, a passerby pointed out how foolish it was "to have a beast of burden and both of you walking." Therefore, the son climbed onto the donkey's back, and he and his father continued on their way.

A few moments later, another passerby said, "Young man, this is so disrespectful. You're riding and your father is walking." Therefore, father and son switched positions, and resumed their journey.

Another passerby had a different take on the situation. He said, "Sir, this is child abuse. Your son is walking, and you're riding."

The only solution seemed to be for both of them to ride the donkey, along with the produce. But before they reached market, the poor donkey dropped dead.

So, the moral of the story is this: You can't please everyone — and if you try, you'll lose your ass in the bargain.

This is a lesson that I'm still learning — but it's ever true for a conductor. Conducting has never been a democratic process. If it were, it would lead to a revolution. I don't believe the creation of any great lasting art takes place in chaos.

Marlee Matlin, an actor with whom I have worked with many times at Epcot, puts it this way:

"I have made the choices that work best for me. I know I cannot please everyone, and that's fine."

Flashing for Jesus

"No one can serve two masters, for either he will hate the one and love the other, or he will be devoted to the one and despise the other."
—*Matthew 6:24*

I believe I can keep numerous plates spinning at one time. But I've learned that trying to multitask can have unfortunate results, and that no one probably does it as well as they think — including me.

When Taylor, my son, was a small child and just starting to walk, I was at home waiting on a repairman, watching my son and studying Mozart's Requiem for an upcoming performance. My wife Gail was gone, and I had just gotten out of the shower.

I heard the doorbell ring, so I threw on a robe, picked up Taylor out of his crib, grabbed my Mozart score, and along with Mac, my little Scottie, we ran to the door.

Sadly, it wasn't the repairman, but two ladies from Jehovah's Witnesses. In order to open the door and receive their literature, I sat Taylor down and tucked my score under my elbow.

Just as I reached for the ladies' pamphlet, Taylor and Mac bolted for the door. As I lunged to keep them in the house, my music fell to the floor, and my robe fell wide open.

What do you say when you've just flashed two Jehovah's Witnesses? All I could think of was, "Excuse me!"

It would have been prudent for these two women to heed the advice given in Proverbs 4:25: *"Let your eyes look directly forward, and your gaze be straight before you."*

Musician's Creed

"Time is what we want most, but what we use worst."

—*William Penn (1644-1718)*

"Early is on time, on time is late, and late is unacceptable." These are words to live by, if you're to be successful in the music business — or, for that matter, in most jobs.

In my first teaching job, I challenged the aforementioned maxim. School started very early. My report time was 7:10 a.m., and I had a 30-minute drive to get there. Luckily, I didn't have a first-period class, so I had time to wake up. Remember, I'm a certifiable night-owl, so those early mornings were grueling.

My first semester was quite successful, and I had just started my second semester. It was time for my annual review by the administration.

It was a glowing review. However, at the end of the meeting the principal said, "Let's talk about your first period of the day." I replied, "I don't have a first-period class." The principal noted that I would wander in a bit late some days, and insisted that even though I didn't have a class, I needed to be on time.

"You may be the best music teacher I've ever supervised, but rules are rules," he stated. "You will show up on time, or I won't renew your contract. There are no exceptions. And while you might be a rising star, it's even more important you play by the rules."

This was a great lesson for a young teacher, and it made a huge impression. Throughout my career since then, I've always been a stickler for starting and ending on time.

I find it insulting to the musicians in front of me to be cavalier with their time in rehearsals. Members of the Bach Festival Choir travel from nine different counties — some for several hours — to participate in rehearsals. So disrespecting their time would be bad form indeed.

The same principle applies to a professional orchestra rehearsal, but also remembering that's it's like a taxi — the meter is always running.

Our average rehearsal call is 150 minutes with a 20-minute break, so you must plan carefully. I learned a lot during my first orchestra rehearsal for the Bach Festival Society. I lectured for some time about the origins of the work, and then asked, "Are there any questions?"

The sardonic concertmaster raised his hand and said, "Are you in two or four?" Point taken — let's get to work.

My education continued the next day at lunch with Mr. John Tiedtke, President of the Bach Festival Society. He thought it had been a good rehearsal, but said he had a comment and then a question.

He agreed that my explanations about the music were interesting. But, he asked, were they worth $60 per minute? "I guess the answer is no," I replied. He nodded and said, "Remember that you're spending our donors' contributions, so be a good steward."

Ever since that discussion, I approach the organizational structure of a rehearsal with a commitment to efficiency. I try not to have much idle time in rehearsals, and not just for cost reasons. Whenever I stop a musical ensemble, I recognize that I only have a few seconds to comment before the rehearsal's momentum is interrupted.

It's guaranteed that if too much time passes, someone will fill the silence with sound. This means I must know what I'm going to say before I stop — and I've learned not to stop unless I can address the problem.

There are also times when a good laugh or a pause is needed. Just as sorbet cleanses the palate, a well-timed interruption can put a rehearsal back on track.

Trying to be efficient is demonstrating respect not only to the musicians in front of the podium, but also to those patrons behind the podium who make our work possible and rewarding.

"Your time is limited, so don't waste it living someone else's life. Don't be trapped by dogma — which is living with the results of other people's thinking. Don't let the noise of others' opinions drown out your own inner voice. And most important, have the courage to follow your heart and intuition."

—Steve Jobs (1955-2011)

Mac

"If there are no dogs in Heaven, then when I die I want to go where they went."

—Will Rogers (1879-1935)

It's amazing to me why anyone would have an ugly dog when they could have a Scottie. Bias acknowledged.

When I find something I like, I tend to stick with it. That's precisely why I've owned six Scottish terriers — and all five of my male Scotties have been named Mac.

I've shared my life with other breeds, including a great little westie named Sam and, as a child, a bulldog named Suzie, and a cocker spaniel named Whimpy. But my current Scotties, Abby and Mac, are the "cat's meow." Pun intended.

Scottish terriers are not the most cooperative of dogs. The breed is self-assured, smart, and independent — just the way I like my dogs, and my students for that matter.

My Scotties have all had similar characteristics, yet each a very distinct personality. They've been "Mac Gruff," "Mac Sweet," "Mac Weird," Mac Genius," and now "Mac Joyful." An old Scottish proverb perfectly describes my philosophy of dog selection: "Be slow in choosing a friend, but slower in changing him."

I associate my late-night musical score study sessions with my Macs, because all of them have sat near me as I've practiced and studied. And never once have they barked in disapproval, or offered judgment of me or the music.

All I know is that in my next life, if I'm reunited with my Scotties, it will be certain that I've made it to Heaven.

"If you pick up a starving dog and make him prosperous he will not bite you. This is the principal difference between a dog and man."

—Mark Twain (1835-1910)

Angels and Angel Food Cake

"Music has been called the speech of angels; I will go further, and call it the speech of God himself."
—*Charles Kingsley (1819-1875)*

My grandmother, Agnes Stewart Jackson, had a profound influence on me. She was the daughter of a coal miner, and both of her parents were poor Scottish immigrants.

She was an eternally kind person and a faithful believer, as confirmed by a letter I have, congratulating her on 60 years of perfect attendance at her home Methodist church.

My grandmother had a joyful heart, she was always singing — although not especially well — and she lived to help others. The people in her small Missouri town lovingly nicknamed her "Aunt Aggie."

When she learned that I was going to make my living as a musician, she shook her finger at me and said, "God gave you that talent. So you'd better be somewhere on Sunday morning using that gift."

Since I conduct a great deal of sacred music, and have served First Congregational Church of Winter Park for 30 years, I hope to have gotten a "pass" in her eyes.

The day my grandmother passed from this world, we received a small angel food cake in the mail. She had baked it a few days before to celebrate my daughter's first birthday.

That cake has been in our freezer for 28 years. I don't have the heart to toss it.

I feel that my grandmother passed her servant heart to my daughter, Kaley, that day. I know she's the one who taught me about sharing and being a gentleman. In my life, she epitomized unconditional love.

My grandmother was a wonderful person, although her life was lived without fanfare. It seems that many of us swing for the fences instead of being willing team players who realize that any good we do can make a big difference.

She had "being happy in your own skin" down to an art form. Her life reminds me of Ralph Waldo Emerson's statement:

"To laugh often and much; to win the respect of intelligent people and the affection of children; to earn the appreciation of honest critics and to endure the betrayal of false friends; to appreciate beauty; to find the best in others; to leave the world a bit better whether by a healthy child, a garden patch or a redeemed social condition; to know even one life has breathed easier because you have lived. This is to have succeeded."

The 13th-century Persian Islamic scholar, Rumi, said, "There are many ways leading to God, and I have chosen the way of music…".

If the 14th chapter of Revelation is accurate, and music is being played and sung in Heaven, and — the big if — if I'm fortunate enough to get there, I'm confident that my grandmother will greet me. And expect me to be ready to go to work.

"Music is a sublime art precisely because, unable to imitate reality, it rises above ordinary nature into an ideal world, and with celestial harmony moves the earthly passions."

—Gioachino Rossini (1792-1868)

Describing the Indescribable

"Aesthetes have it all over intellectuals in one very important respect: You'll rarely catch us hustling anyone off to the nearest guillotine. We're too busy trying to make the world more beautiful. Our hands are stained with ink and paint, not blood."

—Terry Teachout (b. 1956)

Writing about music is much more problematic than making music — and describing an aesthetic experience is nearly impossible. Philosophers should stop reading this essay now, because my explanation of aesthetics isn't textbook.

One more disclaimer: I'm sorry if this feels a bit new-agey. Remember, I was a child in the '60s and a teenager in the '70s.

To make a judgment on aesthetic value is a matter of taste, and when you try to describe that judgment, words never seem adequate. But let me try....

In music, taste is a personal choice that can change and be individualized through familiarity, education, and cultural considerations. So for someone to share the experience means the emotions, senses, and intellect must all agree on what is beautiful.

Multiply that by a choir and orchestra, and I think you'd have a better chance of being hit by lightning than for all involved to feel that they're experiencing beauty simultaneously. That said, such experiences actually happen — and when they do, "Music echoes the magic and mystery of the universe," says author Jan Swafford.

We musicians aren't in the best seats to enjoy the aesthetic experiences we're trying to provide. We're focusing, and not free to imagine and absorb sound without the self-evaluation of all that is technical and expressive at the moment. We're constantly examining pitch, tone, rhythms, blend, and so forth.

Still, I've been blessed on a number occasions to have music-making cause the kind of indescribable pleasure for me that I hope it does for the audience. When that happens, you become a bit like a junkie wanting the next fix.

But the Muses parcel these experiences out judiciously. I believe that such occurrences are only possible if the following are present: technical and musical command of the score, total immersion and submission to the power of music, and the freedom to become selfless in the sound.

Only then can the spiritual aspects of music take charge and whirl around, above, and through you. When it does, you'll spend the rest of your life chasing after another such sensory overload.

"Music gives a soul to the universe, wings to the mind, flight to the imagination, and life to everything."
—Plato (4th century B.C.)

Music for the Heart

> *"Some kinds of music dissipate in seconds.*
> *Other kinds remain a lifetime,*
> *Stored in the limbs, or maybe the brain, or even the heart."*
> —*Derrick de Kerckhove (b. 1944)*

The first concert in my first Bach Festival opened in the magnificent Knowles Memorial Chapel with Bach's Orchestral Suite #3. This is the orchestral suite that features the famous Air on a G String. (The movement has nothing to do with a G string, but the explanation could be longer than the story.)

We had just completed the Overture of the Orchestral Suite. I raised my arms to start the Air, when I saw the principal trumpet player aggressively motioning me to stop.

As I slowly dropped my arms, he twitched his head to encourage me to look to my right. I saw a lot of commotion, with a man lying on the floor and people gathering around him. Naturally everything else in the Chapel came to a halt.

In the distance, I could hear the siren of an ambulance en route. Soon paramedics had pulled a screen around the prone figure, and we heard a defibrillator. This continued for several minutes.

Once the paramedics rolled the stretcher out of the Chapel, people began to settle back in. But what should we do? Take a break? Start with the Overture again? Or proceed to the Air?

We decided to continue with the Air. As you might imagine, there was quite a hush in the building as we began. Because the music was meditative, it seemed the respectful thing to do — and I hoped it would allow the audience members to regain their composure as well.

The man had suffered a heart attack. Gratefully, he made a full recovery.

What occurred to me later is that if one were to have a heart attack, one could do worse than experiencing it in a beautiful chapel, listening to the music of J.S. Bach, with a cardiologist sitting in the next row, and an emergency-room physician in the choir.

"Music speaks ... what cannot be expressed soothes the mind and it gives it rest, heals the heart and takes it whole, flows from Heaven to the soul."

—Anonymous

Chapter 4

America the Beautiful

"America is a tune. It must be sung together."
—Gerald Stanley Lee (1862-1932)

More than two decades ago Dr. Hugh McKean, the past president of Rollins College and founder of the Charles Hosmer Morse Museum of American Art in Winter Park, which holds the largest collection of Tiffany art in the world, called a meeting to organize a July 4th celebration in honor of the opening of the new museum building.

Dr. McKean said he envisioned a small-town July 4th event with first-class talent. He looked at me with a smile and said, "Now, John, you must certainly know what a small-town July 4th celebration in the middle of America looks like."

I responded by saying the same thing I say every year during the event, now an annual tradition in Central Park in Winter Park: "You don't have to work hard to get a boy from Independence, Missouri to wave the flag — so count me in."

In Independence, we had a small-town fair with hot dogs, popcorn, cotton candy, watermelon, and soft drinks, along with such games as sack races, a seed-spitting contest, face painting, and more. It was the epitome of Americana, and attending it felt a bit like walking into a Norman Rockwell painting.

The City of Winter Park continues to sponsor this annual event. And members of the Bach Festival Choir, which is filled with good Americans of all backgrounds, sing patriotic favorites accompanied by a brass choir.

Every year, we sing patriotic standards — and I'm always struck by the power of the lyrics. During every performance, I'm reminded of what Ralph Vaughan Williams said: "The art of music, above all arts, is the expression of the soul of a nation."

Some of the lyrics that especially speak to me are:

"America the Beautiful"

O beautiful for heroes proved, in liberating strife, Who more than self their country loved, and mercy more than life!

"God Bless the USA"

And I'm proud to be an American, where at least I know I'm free. And I won't forget the men who died; who gave that right to me.

"God Bless America"

Land that I love, stand beside her and guide her, thru the night with a light from above.

"This is My Country"

Land of my choice. This is my country. Hear my proud voice! I pledge thee my allegiance, America, the bold. For this is my country, to have and to hold.

"The Star Spangled Banner"

O say does that star-spangled banner yet wave, O'er the land of the free and the home of the brave?

A favorite conducting story involves Toscanini and the NBC Orchestra while touring South America. After an arduous trip, the maestro asked the players to assemble. While they were a bit disgruntled, the dutiful musicians knew better than to complain.

Once they all arrived, Toscanini raised his arms and said, "Happy 4th of July!" Then he led them through a spirited rendition of "The Star Spangled Banner" before giving them the day off.

My patriotism isn't complicated. Frankly, it's rather simplistic, and perhaps even naïve. But it makes sense to me. You may have noticed that I'm drawn to the selfless part of being American. And I'm thankful for those who served in our military and continue to protect the freedom we take for granted.

President Harry Truman expressed it this way: "America was not built on fear. America was built on courage, on imagination and an unbeatable determination to do the job at hand."

I still get goosebumps when performing patriotic music, and feel blessed to have a chance to express my love for country. I only hope to live up to this wonderful quote by Abraham Lincoln: "I like to see a man proud of the place in which he lives. I like to see a man live so that his place will be proud of him."

"The Strongest and Sweetest songs yet remain to be sung. I see America go singing to her destiny."
—Walt Whitman (1819-1892)

Dr. Mann the Man

"A true teacher is one who, keeping the past alive, is also able to understand the present."
—*Confucius (551-479 B.C.)*

During the first Bach Festival that I conducted, it was clear to me that to reach my fullest potential for this esteemed group, I needed more knowledge.

At lunch with the society's president, John Tiedtke, I said, "I attended all my classes and have a good education, but the Bach Festival Society needs a Baroque specialist — and I'm a general surgeon."

Mr. Tiedtke asked, "What do you have in mind?" I suggested that I invite the festival's lecturer, Dr. Alfred Mann, to spend a month with us during a future festival.

When the current festival was over, on the way to the airport to drop Dr. Mann off, I floated my idea of him coming to Winter Park for an extended period of time.

He held up his two palms and said, "Let's see ... would I prefer February in Florida or Rochester, New York? I think we can work something out."

I've never been one to attend seminars, and I've never thought of myself as much of a joiner — though I belong to a number of organizations. In general, though, I agree with Groucho Marx, who famously said that he would not belong to any organization that would have him as a member.

That said, I've always sought out people who knew what I should know.

Over the next four festivals, Dr. Mann spent approximately a month each year, attending all my rehearsals and performances, allowing me to discuss ideas for programming and meeting with me regularly.

He helped me prepare Bach's "Big Three": the St. Matthew Passion, St. John Passion, and the B Minor Mass. We also worked on two orchestral suites, two Brandenburg concerti, and the re-creation of the St. Mark Passion, among other works.

I truly received a post doctorate in the music of J. S. Bach and the Baroque Era.

The debriefing of every rehearsal and concert was a privilege that few conductors ever experience. Years later, I discovered that Dr. Mann was also a consultant to the conductor Robert Shaw.

In subsequent years, we brought Dr. Christoph Wolff to the festival to lecture and conduct — and for me to pick his brain.

Dr. Wolff is brilliant and his knowledge is encyclopedic. His introductions to the festival's 75th anniversary history book tells you what he thinks of us:

"At the time (1935), Winter Park represented a genuine milestone in the cultivation of Bach's music in the United States ... Moreover, its genuine pioneer spirit eventually set the stage for other Bach festivals in the United States because it had demonstrated the attractive variety of Bach's rich vocal and instrumental repertoires, their aesthetic appeal, spiritual dimension, and multi-faceted education function ... May this spirit thrive 'ad multos annos.' "

I may well be one of a few who have worked closely with both of these musicological heavyweights. And if I could sum up in one phrase what I learned from them it would be this: "Trust your instincts, but do your homework."

Too often, it seems that the way in which one becomes an expert is to declare oneself to be an expert. Or, as Oscar Wilde defined the term, an expert is simply "an ordinary man away from home giving advice."

Neither, Dr. Wolff or Dr. Mann would want to be referred to as experts. Dr. Mann once said to me, "It would be difficult to call yourself a Bach scholar and truly be one." A lesson offered and learned about humility and grace.

Following Dr. Mann's fourth month-long visit to Winter Park, I wrote him my annual thank-you note. In it I joked that "I should ask you to confirm I have earned a post-doctorate from your tutelage." In that same correspondence, I expressed regret he wouldn't be with us for next year's B Minor Mass.

In a return letter, Dr. Mann reminded me that the first publisher of the B Minor advertised it as "the greatest work ever written." Then he went on to say:

"You will experience again how right he was! I will miss you as I will miss the Mass, but I will be with you in spirit every minute you rehearse and perform the great work, and I know what a wonderful performance it will be! I know that, this time, it would be the teacher learning from the student."

Rest in peace — and thank you, Dr. Mann.

"Learning is the only thing the mind never exhausts, never fears, and never regrets."
—Leonardo da Vinci (1452-1519)

Critics Can Be Like Eunuchs

"Critics are men who watch a battle from a high place, then come down and shoot the survivors."
—*Ernest Hemingway (1899-1961)*

A number of years ago, we had a music critic in Orlando who didn't seem to like music very much. He was, thankfully, nothing like our current critic. Along with most of the other musicians in town, I endured his mean-spirited, often sarcastic attacks.

One day at a gathering after a concert, a patron asked me if I'd like to comment publicly on the one of the critic's recently published reviews. My response was that I agreed with Brendan Behan, the Irish poet and playwright, who said, "Critics are like eunuchs in a harem; they know how it's done, but they're unable to do it themselves."

I later discovered the critic was also in attendance at that gathering.

A few weeks later, at lunch with Fred Rogers of Mister Rogers' Neighborhood fame, I asked him how he dealt with criticism that he deemed unfair or uninformed.

His response changed my professional outlook. He said, "Pity a person who can't find joy in making music like you do." That's all well and good, I said, but it still isn't fair. "Trust and believe in yourself," Fred replied. "You know when things are good. Right will prevail."

The problem with being consistently criticized is that it can make you question your ability and knowledge. For many years, I kept a quote from author Honore de Balzac close at hand: "When you doubt your power, you give power to your doubt."

Mozart believed in himself regardless of criticism. He revealed, in a letter to his sister, how he was able to do so: "I don't pay attention to anybody's praise or blame. I simply follow my own feelings."

My response to criticism, in general, has been to work harder and to take responsibility. Experience has allowed me to know that no self-respecting musician should let a critic be more important than the music-making itself.

Matthew 24:13 reminds us, "The one who endures to the end will be saved." But the gospel according to this John says, "I'm still here, and the critic is gone."

"Pay no attention to what the critics say; no statue has ever been put up in honor of a critic."
—Jean Sibelius (1865-1957)

Blowin' in the Wind

"Music happens to be an art form that transcends language."
—*Herbie Hancock (b. 1940)*

Many years ago, I took a group of Rollins College students to Italy. In addition to attending many formal concerts, we sang for the students of Julius Caesar Middle School in Mestre, which is near Venice.

After we had finished performing, the young Italian students asked if they could sing for us. With their sweet voices, in broken English, they sang Bob Dylan's anti-war anthem "Blowin' in the Wind."

Let me refresh your memory of the last verse of these lyrics:

Yes, how many times must a man look up,

Before he can see the sky?

How many ears must one man have,

Before he can hear people cry?

How many deaths will it take till he knows,

That too many people have died?

The answer my friend is blowin' in the wind

The answer is blowin' in the wind.

It took the children of Italy to remind me of what Henry Wadsworth Longfellow said more than a century ago: "Music is the universal language of mankind."

"The language of music is common to all generations and nations, it is understood by everybody, since it is understood with the heart."
—*Gioachino Rossini (1792-1868)*

Messiah — One Row at a Time

"I should be sorry, my Lord, if I had only succeeded in entertaining them; I wish to make them better."

—*George Frederic Handel (1685-1759)*

Messiah is standard repertoire for conductors of oratorios and in most cases, for classical vocal soloists. One of the finest tenors I ever had the honor of working with, David Gordon, must have sung hundreds of Messiahs during his career. But what happened during his opening recitative and aria during a performance I conducted of the Messiah Choral Society in Orlando was, I'm sure, a first.

The work begins with a short overture. Then the tenor sings a celebrated recitative and aria, "Comfort Ye" and "Every Valley Shall Be Exalted." I looked at David during the recitative, and noticed that his eyes appeared moist, as though he was about to cry. A moment later I saw tears running down his face.

I couldn't imagine that this was an emotional response to the music. The Christmas card that I'd received from him the year before showed David standing on an Olympic-type platform, holding a trophy with a caption declaring him the winner of "The Messiah-thon."

At the intermission, I couldn't wait to hear what had caused David to become so emotional. Offstage, he broke into laughter as he recounted what had transpired.

During the recitative, he said, a man dragging three small

children — to whom he was apparently determined to impart culture — had climbed over other audience members while working their way to the front row of the Bob Carr Auditorium.

The hall's front row is very close to the stage, forcing people occupying those seats to look almost directly up. As the singing continued, the father apparently decided that he and his brood were too close. So they stood up and climbed again over a row of chairs.

The tears streaming down David's cheeks were caused by fighting back laughter, and tears were his only recourse. By the way, the man and his children got up and left in the middle of another aria before intermission. The necessary cultural exposure had apparently been achieved.

During that same performance, I, too, had a bit of a start. The score I use is loose leaf, so I can add or remove movements as needed. That afternoon, when I turned the page for the last chorus, "Worthy is the Lamb," the music wasn't there. I'd left the score to the last 10 minutes of the work backstage.

I've always preached to my conducting students that a score is only a crutch — and if they can't conduct a piece without it, then they probably don't know the piece well enough. Lucky for me, I knew "Worthy is the Lamb."

"When we sing (from Messiah) 'All we, like sheep, have gone astray,'

might we please have a little more regret and a little less satisfaction?"

—Sir Thomas Beecham (1879-1961)

Heaven Can Wait

"The connections we make in the course of a life — maybe that's what Heaven is."
—Fred Rogers (1928-2003)

The fall of 1990 was a challenge, professionally and personally. It was my first semester as Department of Music Chair at Rollins College, and my first semester as Artistic Director and Conductor of the Bach Festival Society.

My mother had retired the past spring after a long teaching career. It was mid-September, and she and my father had come for a short visit to see the grandchildren.

A few days after they arrived back home, I got a call from my father. He told me that my mom had suffered a small stroke, and that she was having tests run to determine the cause.

What the physicians discovered was an aggressive malignant brain tumor. The next few months were agonizing, as we watched her diminish until her death in mid-November at age 61.

I saw my mother often during her last two months. During my final visit, a few days before her death, she wasn't cognizant. But as I said my goodbyes, I kissed her forehead and whispered in her ear, "I love you and I will see you in Heaven."

We live in a time where the congregations of many mainstream Protestant churches are shrinking, and there seems to be an increase in secularism and non-believers.

I've listened to many scientists, and have been told that my

Christian faith is archaic. It's true that my answers to life's mysteries are few, and I have tons of questions and even doubts.

I've studied the stages of faith by such famed philosophers as Fowler, Piaget, and Kohlberg. They're interesting and helpful, but none capture my belief. Isn't that the very heart of faith — believing what can't necessarily be proven?

I do know that I couldn't be as effective or sincere in interpreting sacred music if I didn't believe in what I was presenting. Many great musicians have been able to do so, but I couldn't deal with being disingenuous.

For instance, how could one look at a creation like the St. Matthew Passion and only be concerned with the historic context, and not the powerful beliefs of J.S. Bach?

What I've neglected to share with you is what happened at the end of my mother's life. It's something that solidified my faith.

While I don't sleep often, or long enough, when I do fall asleep I'm not easily wakened. But on the night my mother passed, I was startled and sat up suddenly in bed.

My wife asked what was wrong, and I replied that my mother had just spoken to me. She said, "I love you and you'll be OK." Not more than a moment later the phone rang, and my father reported to me that my mom was gone.

Draw your own conclusions. I have.

"I'm gonna sing 'til the spirit moves in my heart."
—African-American spiritual

The Word was Made Flesh

"The robe of flesh wears thin, and with the years God shines through all things."
—*John Buchan (1875-1940)*

I've never quite trusted any systems and technologies that reproduce or amplify sound. Early in my career, I learned that a performer is often no better than the equipment of the sound technician.

Suffice it to say, I prefer acoustical performances as a way to control sound, and to make performances more present and less artificial.

In 1888, when Sir Arthur Sullivan first heard a phonograph of his music, he expressed his thoughts to the inventor, Thomas Edison. "For myself, I can only say that I am astonished and somewhat terrified at the result of this evening's experiments," said Sir Arthur. "Astonished at the wonderful power you have developed, and terrified at the thought that so much hideous and bad music may be put on record forever."

At First Congregational Church of Winter Park, we were trying out a new wireless audio system, and all the bugs hadn't been worked out. It was the beginning of Advent season, and we had just sung the beautiful hymn, "Let All Mortal Flesh Keep Silence."

Suddenly, the church's sound system started to pick up signals in the area. At first, all we could hear was static. Then, just before the anthem, a police radio message came across loud and clear.

We heard an arrest for alleged prostitution as the police officer blurted, clear as a bell, his concern about "sexually transmitted diseases."

It's true that fact is always stranger than fiction, because the anthem that day was based on John 1:14, which reads, "The Word was made flesh and dwelt among us."

"The human being is flesh and consciousness, body and soul; his heart is an abyss which can only be filled by that which is godly."
—Olivier Messiaen (1908-1992)

Won't You Be My Neighbor?

"The best way to find yourself is to lose yourself in the service of others."

—*Mahatma Gandhi (1869-1948)*

Having conducted more than 800 shows for Disney, one of my favorite memories involves Fred Rogers, known to generations as TV's Mister Rogers. One evening in 2002, my wife Gail brought Fred and his wife Joanne to see the Epcot Candlelight Processional, because Fred wanted to visit actor and literacy advocate LeVar Burton, who was the narrator that evening.

As they got out of the car in the backstage area of Epcot, Fred asked Gail what was taking place in the large tent adjacent to the parking lot. That's where I was rehearsing the choir, she said. Fred asked if he could go watch.

Just a few minutes before, LeVar had visited the tent to greet the students who were singing that night. When he appeared, they sang the theme song to his TV show Reading Rainbow.

Minutes later, Mr. Rogers walked into the same tent, and 300 high school students went ballistic. Without saying a word, Fred walked up to the microphone and began to softly sing "Won't You Be My Neighbor?". Within a few seconds, everyone joined in. When the song ended, Mr. Rogers said, "Sing well, my dears," and left with no ceremony.

It immediately occurred to me that these students, within a short time, had the good fortune of seeing two of the most influential celebrities and educators of our time. Later that evening, I took a picture of Fred and LeVar when they visited backstage.

Fred passed away the following year. When I presented that picture to LeVar a few years later, tears welled up in his eyes. He told me that he'd always wanted a picture with Fred, because Fred was one of his true heroes.

Isn't it amazing — the power of one soft, kind voice? Fred lived by the verse, "Love does no harm to a neighbor; therefore love is the fulfillment of the law." (Romans 13:10).

Every day of his adult life, Fred carried in his wallet a picture of a plaque he saw when he was a student at Rollins. It read, "Life is for service."

The example that Fred set for us demonstrates that love is indeed the answer — and that being a good neighbor is important work.

Maybe Mother Teresa said it best: "We cannot all do great things, but we can do small things with great love."

"Music is the voice that tells us that the human race is greater than it knows."
—*Marion C. Garretty*

Keep His Beard

"There is always a period when a man with a beard shaves it off. This period does not last. He returns headlong to his beard."

—*Jean Cocteau (1889-1963)*

Nearly 20 years ago, I received an unexpected call from a music director at Walt Disney World. He said they had a proposition for me, and wondered if we could meet to discuss it. I agreed, and arrived at the appointed time and location.

What I expected was a proposal about arranging academic college credit for Disney's summer collegiate music programs. Instead, they asked if I'd like to substitute for the conductor of Epcot's Candlelight Processional program.

"What's the Candlelight Processional?" I asked. They explained that it was a program of carols with full orchestra, a large choir, and a celebrity narrator. I replied that this was right up my alley. They admitted that they knew this was my forte, because they'd just attended a Verdi Requiem I'd conducted a few weeks earlier.

We talked about the expectations. I was told it would only be for one weekend while the primary conductor was working out of town.

I readily and excitedly accepted. As we discussed the particulars, one of them casually mentioned that "Of course, you'll need to shave your mustache and beard."

"You're pulling my leg, aren't you?" I asked. They replied that it was company policy: no facial hair. Now, I don't covet my beard — but it made no sense to me to shave for three days, or one weekend, of conducting.

So, after a bit of thought I said, "Thank you very much for the offer, but I don't think I want to shave, so I am afraid I'll need to pass." We shook hands and I said that if I could ever be of help, to please call on me again. I'd love to be associated with Disney, I said.

A week or so later, I got a call from Rich Taylor, the Vice President of Entertainment for Walt Disney Company. After exchanging pleasantries, he asked if I would consider being a consultant. I said, "Sure, but what does a consultant do?"

After a rather lengthy pause, he said, "Keep his beard."

"Seize opportunity by the beard."
—Bulgarian Proverb

Chapter 5

Even When God is Silent

"God is our refuge and strength, an ever-present help in trouble."

—Psalm 46:1

On the morning of 9/11, I was teaching a class entitled "The Marriage of Music and Poetry." Our topic that day was the World War I poetry of Wilfred Owen.

An assistant came into our classroom and said, "You won't believe this — someone just flew a plane into one of the World Trade Center towers." We stopped our discussion, turned on the TV in the classroom, and watched in horror as the second plane flew into the second tower.

We, along with the rest of the world, realized that this was no accident.

Like everyone else, we were frightened and confused. But I've never been so grateful for the gift of music, because a few hours later there was a choir rehearsal.

For our sake, I knew we needed to make music and sing. From the choral library, I pulled a piece called "Even When God Is Silent." My students needed to feel like a family, and I understood that there's nothing that can elevate the human spirit and soul as much as music.

Poet Robert Browning reminds us that, "Who hears music, feels his solitude peopled at once."

The poem on which "Even When God Is Silent" was based

was found by Allied troops on the walls of a basement in Cologne, Germany. It had been written by someone hiding from the Gestapo. It reads:

I believe in the sun even when it is not shining.

And I believe in love even when feeling it not.

And I believe in God even when God is silent.

We sang this powerful piece several times. Then, with tears in our eyes, we went our separate ways. But I'll never forget that day, and how music moved us from feelings of fear all the way to hope.

"When I hear music, I fear no danger. I am invulnerable. I see no foe, I am related to the earliest times, and to the latest."

—*Henry David Thoreau (1817-1862)*

Better From the Backside

"Don't worry when you are not recognized, but strive to be worthy of recognition."

—Abraham Lincoln (1809-1865)

One evening as I was leaving the stage at Epcot, wearing my street clothes after changing out of my tails, I heard a little boy say to his mother, "There's the conductor." The mom looked at me and said, "No, it isn't." The boy then ran up behind me, looked up at my backside, and yelled to his mom, "See, I told you it's the conductor!"

That's why I've always told my wife Gail that if there's a memorial service for me, please put up a picture that's taken from behind, so people will recognize me.

Denzel Washington said, "Where I think the most work needs to be done is behind the camera, not in front of it."

Conducting is exactly the opposite. For better or worse, the animation that Leonard Bernstein brought to the podium has made conductors a visual part of the concert experience.

However, every orchestral musician knows that audience members rarely see everything that a truly effective conductor is doing. Nuances are taking place, including facial expressions. Eyes and intensity are so crucial to the essence of conducting.

Here, truly the eyes are the windows to the soul. Legendary conductor George Szell told Newsweek magazine, "Conductors must give unmistakable and suggestive signals to the orchestra — not choreography to the audience."

A recent study by Dr. Yannis Aloimonos, from the University of Maryland, discovered that "The more influence of the conductor on the players, the more aesthetically pleasing the music was overall."

Yet a delicate balance is also in play. When a conductor is too much of a "control freak", players don't feel free to emote. Thus, they lose ownership of their respective artistic product — which results in uninspired music making.

There's always been a love/hate relationship between conductors and players — more so in some organizations than others. I'm sure there's a fair amount of "Who does that person think he or she is, to tell me how to play my part?"

Yet, if no one is in charge, the ensemble's music might be comparable to a windsock blowing in front of a used car lot. As the American pianist and comedian Oscar Levant wrote, "A conductor should reconcile himself to the realization that regardless of his temperament, the eventual result is the same — the orchestra will hate him."

My first professional orchestral job was in Kansas City, as a replacement trumpeter in the city's orchestra. I was in the pit playing Offenbach's opera La Pericole. Just before the downbeat, the veteran first trumpet player leaned over and advised that I "quit looking at the conductor, or you're going to get lost."

I've never forgotten that observation, and have spent my whole career trying to be helpful and not in the way.

I'm still in search of the mystical perfect leader-to-servant ratio that an ideal conductor must exhibit. But I do know this — it all begins with being a lifelong learner and respecting the talent in front of you, while always remembering that the audience completes the circle of creativity.

I started this story talking about being watched from behind. But Ralph Waldo Emerson's more philosophical statement says it all: "What lies behind you and what lies in front of you, pales in comparison to what lies inside of you."

"We do not expect you to follow us all the time, but if you would have the goodness to keep in touch with us occasionally..."
—*Sir Thomas Beecham (1879-1961)*

Freezing in Salzburg, and on Fire in Florence

"Cold! If the thermometer had been an inch longer we'd have frozen to death."
—*Mark Twain (1835-1910)*

Many times, I've taken collegiate groups on performance tours, and some of my most memorable ones involve being in Europe during the month of January.

One particular trip was with a chamber choir. We performed and listened to great music in the historic cities of Salzburg, Munich, Vienna, and Prague — all phenomenal cities with thriving cultural offerings.

At a historic cathedral in Salzburg, we presented a concert as part of a church mass. As is the case with historic churches in Europe, the buildings are not well heated, if they're heated all. It was January, and the students and I had been sightseeing all day in the frigid weather. We were hustling to make it the church on time.

As we sat shivering in the pews, waiting for the place in the service when we were to sing, the priest made some comments — in German, of course — and then the congregation looked at us and laughed.

I leaned over to our tour guide, who offered an interpretation: "We should hurry up and let the Americans sing before they freeze and die." We did sing that evening — and we took a number of tunes at especially brisk tempi.

Another study trip took us to Italy, where the goal was to

perform works from the Renaissance and Baroque eras in the original setting.

We sang the music of Giovanni Gabrieli in St. Mark's Basilica in Venice, where we learned how the composer pulled off his famous antiphonal music between the balconies. Then in Siena we sang the music of Andrea Feliciani in the magnificent 14th-century Gothic Cathedral di Santa Maria.

We sang Palestrina, Victoria, and Pitoni in the stunning St. Peter's Altar at the Vatican. But the most educationally enlightening moment took place while rehearsing for a mass in the Cathedral di Santa Maria del Fiore, the "Duomo," in Florence.

While Flemish composer Jacques Arcadelt (1507-1568) was best known for his secular music and for composing for the Sistine Chapel, he spent a short amount of time working in the beautiful Duomo. While there, it's believed that he wrote a lovely little Ave Maria setting.

As we were rehearsing that piece, we noticed that we couldn't manage to sing it in tune. I asked the students why we were unexpectedly having trouble tuning. They said that the echo in the vast cathedral was so strong that the previous chord hadn't dissipated before the next one was sung.

Everyone simultaneously understood the problem and the solution. We slowed the tempo to accommodate the acoustics of the space and — ta-da! — the pitch issues disappeared immediately.

It was a matter of matching the tempo that Arcadelt would have taken when he performed the piece in the 16th century. Experiential education at its best— our brains were on fire, and how cool was that? Very!

"The only source of knowledge is experience."
—Albert Einstein (1879-1955)

Monks Gone Mad

"Man is the only animal that blushes. Or needs to."
—*Mark Twain (1835-1910)*

Carl Orff's Carmina Burana is as rhythmically visceral a work as exists. From the first loud downbeat, with the huge gong attack, this epic has become a 21st-century musical staple.

Orff intended Carmina as a staged work involving dance, choreography, visual design, and other stage action — but most often, it's performed as a cantata with no visual embellishments.

Having conducted Carmina Burana numerous times, both with and without dance, I much prefer it with, or as Orff described, "Theatrum Mundi." That means music, movement, and speech are inseparable.

I went to the professional ballet company in Orlando — then Southern Ballet Theater, now Orlando Ballet — and proposed that we consider combining forces on this masterwork.

They readily agreed, and before we knew it we were onstage ready to give the downbeat for opening night.

The orchestra and I were in the pit, and much of the choir was stationed at various locations in the auditorium. Most were singing from the balcony and watching me on a screen. But about 40 choir members were onstage, dressed in a monk-style "habits" with hoods. The visual effect was striking.

On opening night, as I opened my score, I noticed a bi-folded piece of paper with an image of a female wearing a habit. There was also note reading, "At least three monkettes are *au naturel.*

Their wide smiles will identify them."

I put my hand up to the side of my face to indicate that I wasn't going to look at them. I raised my arms to begin, scanning the set in preparation of the downbeat. Then I noticed that all of the women were smiling broadly. I briefly blushed, then we were off to a fun and exciting performance.

After a good laugh, the next evening I opened my score and saw a similar picture, but this time with a male-looking monk. The inscription read, "The monks wanted equal time. You'll have to guess...."

I can only imagine how bright red my face was that night.

"If you would not be laughed at, be the first to laugh at yourself."
—Benjamin Franklin (1706-1790)

Tickling the Ivories

"The pianoforte is the most important of all musical instruments; its invention was to music what the invention of printing was to poetry."
—*George Bernard Shaw (1856-1950)*

I'm always impressed with world-class artists who perform for the Bach Festival Society. Pianists always hold a special place in my heart because my mother was a pianist. Each of the five artists I wish to discuss here imparted to me an important lesson.

I met the pianist Emanuel Ax late one Sunday morning at Rollins College. We were to select the music he would perform.

The Department of Music is fortunate to have two magnificent Steinway grand pianos, each of which has a unique touch and sound. When pianists come to play, we allow them to select the instrument.

That morning, I unlocked both pianos. Mr. Ax sat down at each keyboard to play on it briefly, and I asked him which he preferred. His response was indicative of his true artistry and confidence.

"Which of the pianos would you like to have moved?" he asked. I assured him that it made no difference to me, and asked if he preferred one over the other. Did he have a favorite? "Yes," he answered. "But it really is up to you."

It was obvious to me that Mr. Ax was so confident in his artistry that he was willing to work with whatever instrument was offered. And he didn't wish to inconvenience his hosts. I was reminded of Bach's statement: "It's easy to play any musical instrument: All you have to do is touch the right key at the right time, and the instrument will play itself."

What a thoughtful and mannerly virtuoso.

***

The Bach Festival Orchestra had just finished rehearsing the introduction to Beethoven's Piano Concerto #5, the composer's popular Emperor Concerto. When soloist Andre Watts entered, I stopped the orchestra and asked, "Is that the tempo you had in mind?"

This was the first time I had conducted this venerable piece, which is a mainstay of Mr. Watts's musical arsenal. Rather than say "no," he politely said, "Well, it's a bit faster than I'm used to, but let's give it a try."

I immediately told Mr. Watts that he was the expert on this work, and asked him to please help us provide the best accompaniment possible through his feedback. He then gave us his tempo, and on we went to inspiring rehearsals and memorable concerts.

Mr. Watts, like Mr. Ax, demonstrated his adaptability and his technical prowess, but did so with consideration. His talent was so immense that he could accommodate others — and his kindness squelched any embarrassment.

***

Another modern piano legend, Paul Badura-Skoda, the author of *Interpreting Mozart: The Performance of His Piano Works*, performed a Mozart piano concerto during the Bach

Festival. He was charming, and his playing was the epitome of eloquence.

Most pianists continue to warm up until right before they come onstage. Mr. Badura-Skoda was featured in the second half of the concert, so he was warming up in the studio of my colleague — and fine pianist — Dr. Gloria Cook.

Because he wished to look his best during his performance, Mr. Badura-Skoda hung up his trousers to avoid wrinkling them as he prepared to perform. Several students walked by Dr. Cook's studio, and looked in the window. There they saw a thin, elderly man playing the piano while wearing his boxer shorts.

We know that news travels quickly, but evidently rumors on a college campus travel even more quickly. Within a few minutes, dozens of students made their way to Dr. Cook's studio to experience the visual.

By the way, when Mr. Badura-Skoda finally played, he looked good and played beautifully. The moral is that one should feel comfortable in one's own skivvies — I mean skin.

***

Charles Rosen, the fine pianist, musical scholar, and author of an influential book, *The Classical Style*, was invited to be a guest lecturer during the Bach Festival.

He agreed, but only if he could also play a piano recital. We hadn't thought of him as a pianist, since at his advanced age he rarely appeared in that capacity.

Yet, Mr. Rosen delivered an evening of brilliance. His playing was impressive — as was his memory — and his insights and commentaries were entertaining and insightful.

How could anyone know so much? Mr. Rosen's encyclopedic knowledge reminded me of the Henry Ford quote, "Anyone who stops learning is old, whether at 20 or 80. Anyone who keeps learning stays young."

Mr. Rosen passed away in 2012, but his command of the music was undiminished in his final years. What a gift to anyone who had the good fortune to hear him.

***

Leon Fleisher is an inspiration on so many levels. He made his debut at age 8, and played with the New York Philharmonic at age 16 under Pierre Monteux, who called him "the pianistic find of the century."

Mr. Fleisher studied with Artur Schnabel, whose pedigree descended to Beethoven through the great pianists Carl Czerny and Theodor Leschetizky.

During the height of his career in 1964, he lost the use of his right hand due to a condition called focal dystonia. He turned his attention to conducting and performing a left-handed repertoire, until injections of botox improved his symptoms to the point where he could again play with both hands.

Mr. Fleisher's recovery didn't happen until the 1990s. So his journey to that time must have been fraught with frustration. Even so, he is recognized as one of the most important piano pedagogues of the 20th century.

When Mr. Fleisher came to perform a Mozart piano concerto with the Bach Festival Orchestra, we began the rehearsal as we would any other with any other guest artist.

I asked Mr. Fleisher if he would mind leading the work from the piano. I knew this was something that he often did, and something to which my orchestra would respond well. But what I learned from the experience was that removing the "middleman" forces the orchestra to listen more closely.

Therefore, the music changed from a traditional concerto sound to that of a more intimate chamber music piece, resulting in a tasteful and compelling reading.

This informed my decision to consider myself as a kind of accompanist when conducting, and to avoid inserting opinions that could interfere with a player's listening. In other words, I serve as a facilitator, or a conduit, so that the artist and the music speak together without an intermediary.

I also had the privilege of working with Mr. Fleisher as he conducted a student performance of Mozart's Symphony #40. I learned that the 2007 Kennedy Center Honoree was not only was a master musician, but an intellectual colossus as well.

The Kennedy Center chairman, Stephen A. Schwarzman, perfectly described Leon Fleisher as "a consummate musician whose career is a moving testament to the life-affirming power of art."

"The art of music is so deep and profound that to approach it very seriously only, is not enough. One must approach music with serious vigor and, at the same time, with a great, affectionate joy.
—*Nadia Boulanger (1887-1979)*

You've Got to
Grow Up Sometime

"We human beings are tuned such that we crave great melody and great lyrics. And if somebody writes a great song, it's timeless that we as humans are going to feel something for that and there's going to be a real appreciation."
—*Art Garfunkel (b. 1941)*

In late December 1998, I was looking forward to meeting and working with Art Garfunkel, who was narrating the Epcot Candlelight Processional for a few evenings.

As I was walking backstage, Mr. Garfunkel approached me and asked, "Are you the conductor here who conducts a lot of the music of Bach?"

I was a bit surprised by the question, but answered yes. He quickly stated that Bach's B Minor Mass "may be one of the best pieces of music ever written."

I quickly replied, "I think you're absolutely right."

Then he said, "You know, you've got to grow up sometime."

Well, now I was dumbfounded. Let's see if I have this correct, I thought. One of the most celebrated singers and musicians of the '60s and '70s — a pop music icon — is talking with reverence about the music of J.S. Bach.

Mr. Garfunkel's comment hit home, as my own musical tastes have evolved over the years. During the next few days, I had a number of conversations with him — often about classical music — and found him to be charming, intelligent, and obviously, a lifelong learner.

> *"Bach belongs not to the past, but to the future — perhaps the near future."*
>
> —*George Bernard Shaw (1856-1850)*

Losing Your Marbles

"Anyone who stops learning is old, whether at twenty or eighty. Anyone who keeps learning stays young."
—Henry Ford (1863-1947)

Every year, I have lunch with our graduating seniors and tell them this story:

A man is riding his horse on a deserted road at night. A stranger appears out of nowhere and asks the rider to dismount and to pick up some stones by the edge of the road.

The stranger says that in the morning, the rider will be both happy and sad. So, the rider picks up a few stones and puts them in his pocket before continuing on his way.

When daybreak comes, the rider reaches into his pocket and pulls out the stones. They're no longer just rocks, but gems — rubies, emeralds, and diamonds. Then he remembers what the stranger had said about being both happy and sad. And he is indeed happy that he stopped – but sad that he hadn't picked up more stones.

To me, the stones represent education and life experiences. My hope is that the story will encourage graduating seniors to be like Michelangelo — who, late in his life, said, "I am still learning."

Next, I have each student select a marble. These aren't ordinary marbles, but clay ones from the late 1800s that came from my grandfather's store.

Just like the students, no two marbles are alike. But they also share similarities. I tell them to keep the marble, and to remember that they're while they're individuals, they're also part of a family and a community.

And if they ever lose their marbles, there are people here who care and will replace them.

Our college family is like the one in Revelation 7:9, "from every nation, tribe, people, and language." I aspire to making the defining characteristic of this family the practice of love.

All of us have a need to feel we're part of something. It's equally important, though, to realize that our very uniqueness has something to offer humanity. Singer Billie Holiday reminds us that, "No two people on earth are alike, and it's got to be that way in music or it isn't music."

Author Annie Dillard wrote, "No child on Earth was ever meant to be ordinary … but then the times get to them, and they wear out their brains learning what other folks expect."

I tell my students that it's only important to be great version of yourself — not a mediocre version of anyone else.

"When I was a child my mother said to me, "If you become a soldier you'll be a general. If you become a monk you'll end up as the pope. Instead I became a painter and wound up as Picasso."

—Pablo Picasso (1881-1973)

Silence is Golden

"A painter paints pictures on canvas. But musicians paint their pictures on silence."
—*Leopold Stokowski (1882-1977)*

We live in a noisy world. The tension created by having sound pound and surround us all day is palpable.

Where musicians get themselves into trouble is trying to fill every second with sound — because the space between the notes is perhaps the most powerful sound we control. Mozart noted that "the silence between the notes is as important as the notes themselves."

A man who lived in silence, the great mime Marcel Marceau, said, "Music and silence combine strongly because music is done with silence, and silence is full of music."

A well-placed pause or silent sigh makes the notes before and after seem all that much more poignant. Likewise, the right amount of time between movements of major works allows the music time to breathe — to use a wine analogy — so the previous movement is completed and prepares you for what is to come.

I think of pauses like punctuation. The beginning and end of a sentence, paragraph, page, or chapter all require a different level of space. I would argue that there are parallels in music, and a conductor has must determine how much space each rest demands.

This leads us to the subjective discussion of interpretation. There's usually not a wrong or right way to interpret a piece of music, because it's unique to you. It changes as you change. The joy of repeating musical works years apart is to see how life has altered your opinions and preferences.

I'm now more patient, and more willing to allow music to breathe and speak for itself.

"There is no such thing as silence. Something is always happening that makes a sound."

—John Cage (1912-1992)

Walking the Walk

"The child is in me still and sometimes not so still."
—*Fred Rogers (1928-2003), from* **The World According to Mister Rogers: Important Things to Remember**

A few remembrances of Mister Rogers:

On January 27, 2001 I found package sitting in front of my office door. Inside it was a note reading, "Happy Birthday Mozart," in the distinctive handwriting of Fred Rogers.

In the package was a "dog-ugly" tie with faces of composers on it. Fred and I "re-gifted" that tie to one another a number of times, each of us claiming it was simply too lovely to accept.

A year earlier, some Rollins College students and I took a trip to Italy, where we sang at the Vatican. In describing the trip to Fred, I told him that students were talking about all the Pope John Paul-related souvenirs offered by nearby vendors.

Some were rather tacky. In that spirit, the students came up with a few products they noticed were absent, such as No Nun Sense Pantyhose, Pope-sicles, and Pope on a Rope soap. The next day, hanging on the doorknob to my office, was soap on a rope with a note from Fred, which read, "You will need to carve it yourself."

Fred was a fine pianist and a wonderful musician. I invited him to a Bach Festival Choir and Orchestra rehearsal, and handed him a score to follow along. I asked him to let me know what he heard. The next morning he returned the score, along with a detailed and precise list of items needing to be addressed. He was right on the money.

It must be a family trait. For many years, my colleague and friend Dr. Daniel Crozier — Fred and Joanne's nephew — has, at my request, attended Bach Festival rehearsals and served as "my ears." His musical insights and keen hearing, like those of his uncle, are remarkable.

Fred and Joanne, along with other friends and colleagues, were at our home for a holiday party. Shortly after they arrived, I noticed Fred wasn't visiting with the other guests. "Joanne, where's Fred?" I asked. She said, "Find your children and he's probably there."

Fred was, indeed, visiting with my children. I said, "Fred, you're off duty." He responded, "I've always loved children more than adults."

At the same gathering, I showed Fred my cufflink collection. He examined at each pair carefully, but appeared to particularly admire one elegant pair with treble clefs on them.

Several years later, we were invited to attend a golden wedding anniversary party for Fred and Joanne in Pittsburgh. What do you give such a famous couple for a present?

I wanted the gifts to be personal, so I gave Joanne a blanket bearing the Rollins seal — they had met here when both were students — and I gave Fred the pair of cufflinks that he seemed to have liked the best.

In 2003, I received a letter from Fred that he had mailed shortly before his passing. Inside was a pair of cufflinks with an owl on them. He had written, "To John, cufflink collector, from X the Owl." (X the Owl was a mainstay on Mr. Rogers' Neighborhood.)

Shortly afterward, a second envelope from Fred arrived. Inside were the cufflinks I had given him, and a note reading, "To

John, my friend, thank you for sharing these with me." You can only imagine how I cherish those cufflinks — and how special it is for me to wear them.

The cufflinks aren't special just because Fred Rogers had worn them. They're special because he thought it was important to return them to me as his time was drawing near. That sort of kindness and consideration of others was so Mr. Rogers.

"Most of us, I believe, admire strength. It's something we tend to respect in others, desire for ourselves, and wish for our children. Sometimes, though, I wonder if we confuse strength and other words—like aggression and even violence. Real strength is neither male nor female; but is, quite simply, one of the finest characteristics that any human being can possess."

—Fred Rogers (1928-2003), from **The World According to Mister Rogers**

Chapter 6

The Ultimate Team Support

"People who work together will win, whether it be against complex football defenses or the problems of modern society."

—Vince Lombardi (1913-1970)

I'm a sports fan, and loved playing sports when younger. Still do! While I marvel at the athleticism of individuals such as Olympians, I especially enjoy team sports, because of the "all for one, one for all" mindset that it takes for a team to succeed.

Certainly, it takes skill and coordination to toss a round ball through a hoop 10 feet in the air, or to kick an oblong ball through goal posts from 40 yards away. But if you love extreme teamwork, then you should consider playing or singing in a musical group.

Take the Winter Park Bach Festival Choir as an example. Having 160 people singing 16th notes at 120 beats a minute — in Latin. Now that's coordination.

One could also make a comparison to batting averages. If a baseball player hits .300, it's an immensely successful season. But if a musician only hits one out of three notes, it's a dreadful performance.

I realize this isn't exactly apples to apples. But it makes the point that teamwork is required to sing or play in an ensemble — and it addresses the expectation of precision.

Building camaraderie, confidence, character, and caring are all values that we hope playing team sports will contribute to the lives of participants.

Making music in an ensemble has the identical attributes and outcomes, but without concussions or ACL injuries. And while singing into your 70s or beyond is very doable, playing football at that age would be downright dangerous.

Musical ensemble participation can be a lifelong avocation — and for my money, it takes teamwork to a new level.

"Music does bring people together. It allows us to experience the same emotions. People everywhere are the same in heart and spirit."

—Henry David Thoreau (1817-1862)

Thanks Belle!
Good work

Committees and Meetings

"God so loved the world that He did not send a committee."
—Anonymous

Anyone who has worked in the academy, non-profits, or churches knows all about meetings and committees. With all three types of organizations in my life, along with board service, I've grown increasingly more impatient with such time-comsuming activities.

Time is truly our most valuable commodity — and my newest goal is to not let these activities squander too much of it.

Certainly, some meetings are imperative, and many committees do important work. But I don't find long meetings to be productive. If the meeting is efficient, an hour ought to be enough.

Experience tells me that those who are insecure in their leadership want to meet often. Every time I'm sitting in a long meeting, I think of the words of musician Henry Rollins: "No such thing as spare time, no such thing as free time, no such thing as down time. All you got is life-time. Go."

My musical training, especially that as a conductor, is contrary to the meeting and committee mentality. I've never believed that creating art-by-committee works.

The role of a conductor is often misunderstood. Waving one's arms looks easy and enjoyable — and I would be lying if I didn't admit that, at times, it is great fun, and it is almost always rewarding.

But what you don't see are the many hours of study before rehearsals begin. Prior to raising your hands to conduct, you should have analyzed the text — including all the harmonic, melodic, and rhythmic structures of the music — and investigated any potential trouble spots.

Understanding how to lead your group through transitions — or, as I call it, connecting the seams — is critical. There are a myriad of musical decisions to be made surrounding proper articulation, phrasing, and style.

British conductor Sir Thomas Beecham once insisted that "There are two golden rules for conducting an orchestra. Start together and finish together. The public doesn't give a damn what goes on in between."

This flippant comment is a bit misleading. But it does emphasize the need to make starts, stops, and all "seams" smooth. To accomplish this, you simply must know what you want to hear before the downbeat.

My natural teaching tendency leans toward using inclusive learning and encouraging dialogue — but this isn't the norm in the world of conducting. A conductor is, in a sense, a dictator, albeit a dictator who is (hopefully) kind and benevolent.

Ultimately, however, decisions surrounding the musical product belong to the conductor. There's no committee at work here, but plenty of teamwork with other musicians who are friends, colleagues, and students. As you walk the lonely musical plank of conducting, if you've done your job well, musicians around you will serve as your safety net.

An apropos quote for conducting is attributed to Thomas

Edison: "Genius is one percent inspiration, ninety-nine percent perspiration."

So, next time you watch a conductor, you may think that he or she seems inspired. Perhaps it's so. But there's not a lot of magic taking place on the podium. Rather, it's the culmination of scholarship, leadership, and hard work.

"A dream doesn't become reality through magic; it takes sweat, determination, and hard work."
—*Colin Powell (B. 1937)*

Magic and More

"Laughter is timeless, imagination has no age, dreams are forever." —Walt Disney (1901-1966)

I regularly conduct a show for Walt Disney World at Epcot. The Candlelight Processional features the Walt Disney World Orchestra, Voices of Liberty (Disney's professional vocal ensemble), a choir comprised of cast members from throughout the company, and numerous visiting high-school choirs from across Florida and the U.S.

The show consists of carols with a celebrity narrator reading the Christmas Story. While each narrator reads the same script and brings his or her own style to the program, there have been some humorous ad libs.

At the end of most of his shows, singer Steven Curtis Chapman said, "In Kentucky we have a saying that if that don't light your fire, your wood is wet."

Actor James McDaniel jokingly expressed an interest in playing in the percussion section of the orchestra, saying, "I've been playing the triangle so long that I played it when it was still a square."

During the performance, the conductor turns to the audience and asks them to join the choir and orchestra in the singing of "Silent Night." One raining, drizzling evening I turned around to face the audience and got so tickled that I could hardly make it through the verse.

This was during the years when most video cameras had a little red flashing light that illuminated when recording. That, combined with the plastic yellow hooded ponchos Disney sold, made the audience look like thousands of ETs.

Several times, narrators have accidently skipped readings. In that case, he or she must go back and read the section that was skipped, or the conductor needs to skip a tune to catch up.

This is crucial, because all lighting cues are synced with the music — and it's not easy to communicate to the orchestra and 300 singers without being able to speak to them. I have an emergency phone on my podium to talk with the booth and discuss how to remedy such snafus. While it's a bit frightening, it makes the show an exciting challenge. Here are some memories of the celebrity narrators with whom I've worked:

David Ogden Stiers would put a handkerchief in my vest pocket, thinking my tails coat needed the added touch.

Neil Patrick Harris went of his way to make the musicians feel appreciated by sharing food with us.

Angie Dickinson jokingly told me that she would like to take me back to L.A. with her, and then said to my wife, "Never mind — musicians get me in trouble."

I'm rarely star-struck, but I must confess to being tongue-tied when introduced to Julie Andrews.

Marlee Matlin embarrassed me by saying that I danced so much on the podium that I could be on Dancing with the Stars.

Suffice it to say, I've been blessed to meet so many interesting people — and I find it refreshing to discover these celebrities are almost always genuinely kind people.

"Music is probably the only real magic I have encountered in my life. There's not some trick involved with it. It's pure and it's real. It moves, it heals, it communicates and does all these incredible things."

—Tom Petty (1950 - 2017)

In All Things Love

"Are there no Moravians in the Moon, that not a missionary has yet visited this poor pagan planet of ours, to civilize (i.e.) civilisation and christianise Christendom?"
—*Herman Melville (1819-1891)*

The Moravian Church (Unitas Fratrum) is one of the oldest Protestant faiths, with origins dating back to the Bohemian Reformation in the 15th century. The Moravians are known for their missionary work, the value they place upon music, and the high quality of their music.

I have great respect for this denomination. And I find it very fulfilling and humbling to be the one asked to interpret and conduct many of the first modern performances of Moravian music written in the 18th and 19th centuries.

I came in contact with Moravian music by digging through the library at First Congregational Church of Winter Park. Then, after learning that the Moravians began the first-ever Bach Festival, I thought that I should learn more about these visionary people.

The week in 1992 I called the Moravian Music Foundation (MMF) to ask if more music like this existed, happened to be the first week on the job for Dr. Nola Reed Knouse, who remains the Foundation's Executive Director.

I imagine she was amused by my question, and invited me to Winston-Salem, North Carolina to look in the archives. In fact, there are literally thousands of pieces of music in the vault, with most of them needing a modern edition and a modern performance.

I subsequently served a few years on the Moravian Music Foundation's Board of Trustees, and became involved in editing many works. I even programed Moravian music during several Bach Festivals.

My association with them ramped up when Thor Johnson, who had been slated to conduct the 1999 Moravian Music Festival, suddenly passed away, and I was asked to fill in. I accepted.

The MMF Website tells the history of these festivals:

"Beginning in the 1930s and 1940s, scholars and musicians discovered a veritable treasure trove of music in the archives of the Moravian Church in America — manuscripts, early printed music, much of it in German. As they explored more, they were awestruck at the quantity of music, and the variety of composers — those known to be Moravian, and those known in wider musical circles."

The Website continues: "Working with American-born-and-trained conductor Thor Johnson (son of a Moravian minister), a group of clergy and laypersons in Bethlehem, Pennsylvania, decided to hold an 'Early American Moravian Music Festival and Seminar' in Bethlehem, Pennsylvania in late June of 1950."

Mr. Johnson, the founding conductor, presided over the first 11 festivals. After his passing, it was decided that he would be the Music Director in perpetuity, and that future conductors could "guest conduct" for only two festivals.

I conducted my first festival in 1999, and was asked to conduct my second festival. In extending me this invitation, Dr. Knouse said, mostly jokingly, "In the spirit of full disclosure, I should tell you we had asked a number of other conductors to conduct additional festivals — but for a variety of reasons none of them lived to do so."

Given that I felt in good health — and my life insurance was paid — I accepted the invitation. When I arrived to lead the next festival, I felt the organizers' sense of relief. We then had a productively joyful week of music-making.

A few months later, I received a wonderful letter from the gathering of the Northern and Southern Provincial Elders Conference of the Moravian Church, which is the American church's governing body. Someone at the meeting stated that "we have found our new Thor." Then the elders invited me to serve as the festival's "continuing conductor."

With gratitude, I immediately accepted — and have loved the affiliation and the people with whom I've worked. My relationship with the Moravians has influenced how my faith and art intersect.

The Moravians have a motto they refer to for how to live one's life. It has always resonated with me: "In essentials, unity; in non-essentials, liberty; and in all things, love."

Please allow me to offer my take on those principles:

In essentials, unity.

After all, we're all members of one race — the human race.

In non-essentials, liberty.

We're all individuals, and need to be respected for who we are, regardless of personal preferences. Live and let live — or just stay in your own lane.

And in all things, love.

Love is the great healer, the great equalizer, and the creator of all things beautiful.

"Vicit Agnus Noster, Eum Sequamur (Our Lamb has conquered, let us follow him)."
— *Inscription on the Moravian Seal*

St. Matthew or St. Matthäus

"If you talk to a man in a language he understands, that goes to his head. If you talk to him in his language, that goes to his ears."
—*Nelson Mandela (1918-2013)*

A long-standing tradition of the Bach Festival Society of Winter Park is to perform the Passions of J.S. Bach in English. The history of this decision goes back to conversations between the great musicologist Paul Henry Lang and our Bach Festival President John Tiedtke in the early years of the Festival.

According to Dr. Lang, the Passions — which were written in Bach's native language, German — should rightfully be sung in the vernacular of the performers. He believed that trying to recreate an "authentic" performance was not possible, and not advisable. Having read a number of Dr. Lang's essays, I can see why we established this practice.

"An argument can be compelling in print, but far less so carried into actual performance, and it may turn out that its historical basis has no relevance," he wrote. "Authentic performances are unattainable because, even in this information-laden age, there is no such abundance of facts on performance practice as would ensure absolute authenticity."

Most choral conductors and musical purists find the practice of not singing in the composition's original language distasteful. My education taught this same philosophy — resulting in hours of explanations to colleagues about why I conduct the Bach Passions in English.

The text matches the music better in the original language. But what you gain is not as much as you give up.

Having experienced Bach's Passions in both English and German, I find that an audience is far more engaged when they're able to understand the magnificent, dramatic text.

Sheer adherence to original performance practices actually limits the work's impact, often making it a museum piece rather than living art. Those who take early performance practice to an extreme may polarize the music.

Also, one can't forget that audiences of today have a different listening perspective than those of early times.

Ever since reading the chapter on the St. Matthew Passion in Herbert Kupferberg's book, *Basically Bach*, I have felt validated. Kupferberg tells the story of conductor Bruno Walter, who came to the U.S. as a refugee from the Nazi regime.

Previously, Walter had performed a yearly St. Matthew Passion at Eastertime in Leipzig. So, for three years during World War II, he conducted uncut English-language performances with the Philharmonic Symphony Society of New York and the Westminster Choir in Carnegie Hall.

Kupferberg expresses his gratitude to Walter, writing that "for at least one young person in that audience, Bruno Walter's St. Matthew Passion in English was an indelible experience, a monument that has lasted a lifetime."

We conductors must simply get over ourselves and realize that we only have two clients: the composer and the audience. We are mere facilitators. Drawing upon and respecting historical concepts in music is surely vital to the performance, but so is interpreting this music for the present.

"Music is the universal language of mankind."
—Henry Wadsworth Longfellow (1807-1882)

Beethoven and Mozart: Cover Your Ears

"If ever there has been a cosmic musical creation, this is it — a score so overwhelming in its vision, and breadth, that it transcends temporal, worldly affairs."
—Martin Bookspan (b.1926)

Beethoven's incomparable Ninth Symphony is an international iconic work that challenges everyone who performs it. The soloists, orchestras, and choirs all find it formidable.

One spring, before a break at a Bach Festival rehearsal, I announced to the orchestra that we would be performing Beethoven's Ninth Symphony in the fall.

As the players began conversing and moving from the stage on break, my longtime concertmaster, Routa Kroumovitch, walked by the podium and said, "You know that is a tough work." I replied that we would be OK.

She responded that she'd played the Ninth dozens of times, and wasn't worried for herself. "It'll be difficult for you," she said. She added that a conductor could truly be said to have "arrived" when he or she can successfully conduct a Beethoven Ninth Symphony.

At the time, I didn't understand her comments. But as I started my score study, I quickly realized that she hadn't overstated the difficulty factor.

Every movement of this great work presents a beautiful and fun challenge. And, of course, you have to do your homework — and not just for the orchestra. Since the Ninth Symphony is an audience favorite, most veteran concertgoers know it well.

The choral singing, while exhilarating, is often referred to as a "scream fest." I usually tell the choir that the Ninth reminds me of the ending of the movie Braveheart, when the actor playing Robert the Bruce says, "You have bled with Wallace, now come and bleed with me."

When fall arrived, I came to rehearsals well prepared — which resulted in a welcome compliment from Routa. But it was the first performance that made my first Ninth memorable.

The large choir doesn't make an appearance until the fourth movement —but when they do appear, it's "game on," especially during the final few minutes.

The soloists that weekend were all veterans of this work, but an important soprano soloist's entrance went awry. That threw off the other soloists' entrances. We caught the mistake, and for the most part, the audience was none the wiser.

When mistakes happen during a live performance, your goal is always the same — try to limit the damage, get back on track as quickly as possible, and above all, keep the mistake from the audience. Once you're back in control, you're free to feel your heart pounding again.

I had a similar incident happen during my first performance of Mozart's C Minor Mass ("The Great Mass"). We ran out of rehearsal time on an aria and never had a chance to run it in its entirety.

During the performance, the soloist leaned over and asked, "Do you know where we are?" I responded, "I was hoping you knew." I quickly suggested that she not sing again, adding, "When I hear a good cadence, I'll bring this runaway train to a stop."

That's exactly what happened. We later discovered that the orchestra's and our soloist's editions didn't match.

Lessons learned: Make sure everyone has the same edition — and don't perform anything you haven't rehearsed all the way through.

What made me most sad was that I saw my life passing in front of my eyes, and it wasn't that interesting. Frankly, I'm thankful for that.

"Play Mozart in memory of me."
—Frederic Chopin (1810-1849)

Authenticity in Music

"A civilized society is one which tolerates eccentricity to the point of doubtful sanity."
—*Robert Frost (1874-1963)*

Collecting historic letters, photographs and autographs is the hobby of an eccentric. It takes one to know one, and I am one.

A few years ago, I began what for me has been a fascinating pastime. I wanted to feel closer to the sources of my musical inspiration. So I began collecting signed letters or photos of important composers, as well as similar items of prominent conductors.

Of course, the source of inspiration is not the composition itself. What exactly inspired the composer? What life experiences did he or she bring to the work? Once the music was complete, how did it become realized?

Composers often entrust their creations to conductors, who are interpreters. And then the forces involved — that is, every person making music — becomes a part of the creation.

The audience serves as a muse, because music made for one's self is greedy; it feels incomplete and unfulfilled. The creative journey from the composer's inspiration to the audience's ears is a sacred one, a covenant of music making.

In addition to musical implications, when I study a historic work, I try to uncover what was happening in the composer's life at the time it was written. I then postulate how those circumstances may have impacted his or her creative process.

Collective wisdom informs our work today. For example, what impression did Bach's St. John Passion have on the choral and orchestral players who first performed this work?

And what did the players learn, or impart to those who heard the performance?

These are the same questions asked by those of us trying to make music come alive today.

Music is a human emotion, raw and unfiltered. If it is too affected or not sincere, audiences can tell. Just as children can spot phonies, an unengaged performer can be found out.

Great music draws emotion from each generation it touches. This is where true authenticity is determined. Not in lowering a pitch or holding a bow a bit differently. These considerations, while important, are mechanical aspects, and curiosities of current practitioners — not necessarily at the core of the art itself.

In music, true art comes not from the instrument, but from the heart and mind of the person playing it.

So why do I collect memorabilia from composers and conductors who first touched the pieces I conduct? Because it makes me feel closer to the art, and to the humanity it represents. It sparks my curiosity and compels me to seek more than superficial knowledge.

Collecting inspires study and reflection, both historically and personally. It forces me to think of those master musicians not as mere historic figures but as people — souls who lived, loved, and breathed, just like me.

By no means am I placing myself in the same league as these musical greats. But I do want to know them better — and in a curious way, I believe they want to know us, too. I believe those who create masterpieces are writing for the ages.

So, when you see my music score on a stand in front of me, quite often you'll also see a letter or photo from the original composer or conductor.

Given all the enjoyment these artists have given and continue to give, they deserve to hear their works from where I stand, and in the spirit of mystical romanticism.

I hope they're enjoying the ride.

"May it go from the heart, to the heart."
—Ludwig van Beethoven (1770-1827)

Sleeping on the Job

"I had a dream that I was awake and I woke up to find myself asleep."

—*Stan Laurel (1890-1965)*

Boy, was I tired!

It was the middle of December on a Sunday evening. The day before, I had conducted a two-and-a-half hour rehearsal of the Bach Festival Orchestra and Choir, a Nutcracker Ballet matinee, a Candlelight Processional at Epcot, and then, to cap it off, one more evening Nutcracker performance.

Just a few days earlier, I had finished the college's Christmas Vespers, the city's Christmas in the Park concert, and a Messiah performance. I was also in the process of planning the Bach Festival's upcoming concerts, while continuing to conduct Candlelight Processionals at Epcot.

This particular Sunday started with a church service, followed by another Nutcracker matinee, and ended with two more shows at Epcot.

The first Candlelight Processional was well performed and wonderfully uneventful. Before the next show, I got a snack and relaxed a bit.

We were about 15 minutes into the last show of the night, performing an arrangement of "Away in a Manger," when I closed my eyes to enjoy the music.

Then I heard a cymbal roll in an unfamiliar place. I must have seemed startled when I looked toward the concertmaster. She mouthed to me, "You were asleep." As I continued conducting, I shook my head in denial. Then I looked at the principal cellist, who nodded her head in confirmation.

As I looked around the string sections, they were all grinning and agreeing with the concertmaster.

I must have dozed off for a short time. The best I can figure, it was around 30 seconds or so.

After the show, I asked the players, "How did I do conducting in my sleep?" One said, "You just kept conducting a three pattern and didn't waver."

Then another said, "Now, don't get the idea we were watching you anyway."

"Even sleepers are workers and collaborators in what goes on in the universe."

—Heraclitus (ca. 5th century B.C.)

Chapter 7

Verdi's Best Opera

When asked about Verdi's Requiem, the famous conductor Hans von Bülow called it "Verdi's latest opera, though in ecclesiastical robes."

Giuseppe Verdi's frequently performed Messa da Requiem, sometimes called the "Manzoni Requiem," is one of the all-time greatest choral works.

Everyone enjoys this work: the singers, players, and audiences — not to mention conductors.

Although it's "sacred music," I believe it's Verdi's best opera.

The work uses the traditional musical setting of a Roman Catholic funeral mass, but it wasn't written for that purpose. Even so, it premiered in 1874 at San Marco Church in Milan. Just three days later it was performed at Milan's La Scala opera house, where Verdi himself conducted it and where he believed it belonged.

Verdi's Requiem was an immediate hit in Paris and other prominent cities in Europe — except for London, where they couldn't even fill the newly built Royal Albert Hall. Londoners, it seemed, couldn't accept a "religious work" performed in a secular venue.

Verdi was a spiritual person, but he wasn't conventionally religious. He walked barefoot for miles as a child to attend church. However, it was more to play the organ than to worship.

When he became famous, Verdi would escort his wife to church, but he would never go in. He wasn't an atheist, but he did seem to be a skeptic.

Verdi infuses the Requiem with awe-inspiring melodies, visceral rhythms, and dramatic tempi and dynamic changes. His ability to write dramatic music is on full display throughout this masterpiece.

The very first time I conducted the Verdi Requiem, I hired Diane Curry, the mezzo-soprano featured on a Grammy Award-winning 1988 recording of the work by Robert Shaw and the Atlanta Symphony.

Not only did Ms. Curry have a powerful voice, she was also fun to work with — and she was fearless. One challenge faced by any conductor of the Requiem is to manage the balance between the orchestra and the soloists. Often, the orchestral parts are so powerful that they can make it difficult for the soloists to be heard.

During a rehearsal, I stopped the orchestra and asked them to play a bit softer so we wouldn't "drown out" Ms. Curry. Before I could finish my request, she chimed in. "No need to do that," she said. "Bring them on, honey. I can sing louder than all of them." And she did.

The second time, a few years later, I was in the middle of conducting the long Dies Irae section when I heard some noise to my left. I turned to see a woman in a wheelchair, tethered to a device that helped her to breathe, talking to an usher.

The usher walked away and the woman remained until the end of the performance. Then she was quickly ushered out of the Chapel.

After the concert, I asked what had happened. Evidently the woman, who was straining to breathe, refused to leave despite her distress. She told the usher that this was her favorite piece of music — and if remaining to hear it killed her, "What a way to go."

Speaking of "What a way to go," a month after Verdi died

in Milan, his and his wife's coffins were moved to their final resting place. Approximately 300,000 people lined the streets — it was Italy's largest-ever state funeral — and 800 sang at the graveside.

Conducting the 800 singers was none other than a man who had played cello in the orchestra for Verdi at La Scala, Arturo Toscanini.

"All true and deeply-felt music, whether secular or sacred, has its home on the heights where art and religion dwell."
—Albert Schweitzer (1875-1965)

Tiffany and Trains

"Our hearts grow tender with childhood memories and love of kindred, and we are better throughout the year for having, in spirit, become a child again at Christmas-time."
—Laura Ingalls Wilder (1867-1957)

It isn't the Christmas season for me until Christmas in the Park.

Imagine a holiday concert under the stars, featuring a fabulous choir and brass ensemble, in a beautiful outdoor setting. Further imagine that you're sitting among of a collection of magnificent, lighted Tiffany windows.

What I just described is the magical annual holiday evening that always takes place on the first Thursday of December in Winter Park. Christmas in the Park was started by Hugh and Jeanette McKean, benefactors of the Charles Hosmer Morse Museum of American Art, in 1979.

It was a perfect way for the McKeans to share some of their rare Tiffany collection with the public in an informal setting. Today, the museum and the City of Winter Park co-sponsor the event.

Christmas in the Park wasn't always so grand. When the Bach Choir started participating, it was held at the far end of Central Park. The singers, standing on temporary bleachers, performed for a modest crowd of a few hundred, at best. There was no instrumental accompaniment.

Also on hand in the early days was a school bus, converted at the behest of Dr. McKean — who was then director of the Morse Museum — into a mobile museum of art. A unique added attraction was Gus the Spitting Camel. No kidding.

It took a few more years to convince Dr. McKean and my Bach Festival boss, Mr. John Tiedtke, to allow us to engage a brass quartet. Over lunch a few years later, I also suggested that we move the event to the north end of the park, to a permanent stage.

Over the years, the event grew and grew. We kept fine-tuning our part of the presentation, but it was the vision of Hugh McKean and his museum staff who made this production more polished and professional every year.

There are a few traditions every year I don't dare change. We always wave at the passengers on the trains that pass by the park. The audience always joins the choir by shaking their keys during "Jingle Bells." At the end of "Silent Night," attendees hold up their illuminated cell phones — a 21st-century version of lighters.

Some people bring snacks and others bring catered meals. Some sit on blankets, and many have staked out areas that they elaborately furnish, almost like outdoor living rooms.

Typically, more than 7,000 people show up. What's best about this event isn't just the music, and maybe not even the beautiful Tiffany windows. It's the sense of community.

Every year, I look out over a vast sea of people enjoying art. But what's especially gratifying is watching folks enjoying one another. Together, we usher in the holiday season.

"A healthy social life is found only, when in the mirror of each soul the whole community finds its reflection, and when in the whole community the virtue of each one is living."

—*Rudolf Steiner (1861-1925)*

Crossing the Bar

"Grief drives men into habits of serious reflection, sharpens the understanding, and softens the heart."
—*John Adams (1735-1826)*

My father's caregiver called me on a Monday morning during a Bach Festival week. She said that my father, who was suffering from dementia, hadn't wanted to get out of bed that morning, and was going to be taken for a medical evaluation.

Every hour or so, I got an update. And things went from bad to worse. I asked if I should be there, and his caregiver said there was no need yet —she would keep me posted.

On Tuesday, he wasn't improving. So I said that I would be there bright and early Wednesday morning. Later on that Tuesday, I was at the podium rehearsing the haunting soprano solo, "Erbarme Dich", from the St. Matthew Passion. The English translation of this text is "For Love My Savior Now is Dying."

As I called for a rehearsal break and checked my phone, I noticed a voicemail message had been left by my father's caregiver. Her message wasn't an update on his condition, as I expected, but news that he had suddenly passed.

I had discovered earlier that death is in no way ceremonial. A year before, I had gone to the hospital to visit a student with a terminal illness and, along with his family, watched this wonderful young man simply slip away.

This experience created an unforgettable image. We all lose

family and friends — and always too soon. There was nothing I could do now.

So I finished the rehearsal and prepared for a longer rehearsal that evening. But I wasn't sure how I was going to make it through. Music always awakens my emotions, and the grief — combined, frankly, with guilt over not getting to my father's bedside in time — was formidable.

What happened at the beginning of the evening's rehearsal, however, was so moving that it allowed me to continue.

Word of my father's passing had spread through the orchestra and to my colleagues. As I walked on stage to begin the rehearsal, the orchestra stood up silently. As I turned away to fight back tears, I noticed most of my colleagues from the Department of Music in attendance, sitting a few rows back.

I walked over and thanked them, but assured them that their presence, while deeply appreciated, wasn't needed. "I'm OK," I said. Gloria Cook spoke for the group, replying, "Yes, it is necessary. You need to know that you're not alone."

More strongly than ever, I felt the love and care of those with whom I make music.

A musical community always responds passionately in such situations. The very fact we're artists means that we lay bare our sorrows and joys to one another, and to the audience, every time we make music.

But the love that surrounds one of their own when that person is hurting is truly beyond description. Only through the strength of my family and colleagues did I make it through the poignant Bach's St. Matthew Passion at week's end.

It has been said that we come into this world alone, and we leave this world alone. But those of us who are truly fortunate are loved when we arrive, and loved when we leave.

I have experienced first-hand, the amazing, healing salve of music.

"For me music is a vehicle to bring our pain to the surface, getting it back to that humble and tender spot where, with luck, it can lose its anger and become compassion again."

—*Paula Cole (b. 1968)*

The Power of Singing

"You can lead a horse to water but can't make him drink."
—Anonymous

"But you can walk that damn horse around the pond until he either drinks or dies."
—E.V. "Buck" Jackson (1902-1977), my grandfather

I can be a bit demanding — let's say insistent — in rehearsals. I call it "consistent persistence." And there are times when a musical issue seems slow to correct. Even though I usually know who the outlier is, I'm careful never to embarrass any individual during rehearsal.

Once I single someone out, the *esprit de corps* is compromised. So I must be okay with the ensemble being perturbed at me, even though my purpose is to help the ensemble deliver its best possible performance.

It's common for me to speak with individuals in private about something I've heard, but public humiliation has diminishing returns, and creates long-term damage to the sound and psyche of a choir.

In my early years with the Bach Festival Choir, I used a rather complex set of signals to let "repeat offenders" know that I was hearing them. There've been times I've felt like a baseball coach giving signals to a choir member to not swing at the next pitch — or, more appropriately, to not sing so loud.

A choir doesn't only build community — it is one. The current trend in choral music of bringing in professional singers has merit, but misses the point of choral singing.

These choirs-for-hire fail to create a group of singers or kindred spirits to feed the community's collective soul. Any veteran choral singer will describe the joy of making music as being a part of something larger than himself or herself.

For me, choral singing is the ultimate soul food.

Research by psychologist Nick Stewart of Bath University indicates that "people who sing in a choir had a stronger sense of being part of a meaningful group, and there is a suggestion that there is something unique about the unified moving and breathing with other people."

Recent studies have concluded that groups of singers sometimes actually synchronize their heartbeats. The medicinal power of singing isn't completely understood, and is difficult to quantify.

But I expect physicians in the future will tell their patients to sing and they'll feel better tomorrow.

There's little challenge in making a choir of paid choral singers sound good, compared the challenge of making a choir of unpaid choral volunteers sound as good as the professionals.

In the Bible, in Corinthians 7:20, the Apostle Paul talks about being contented in one's role in life, and to "bloom where you are planted."

Luckily for me, I've been blessed with the honor of working with wonderful people who love to sing — the best kind of folks. They're wise and caring people who are willing to work for a common goal; people whose selfless singing creates a sea of sound to inspire others.

The Bible verse about not being a prophet in one's own country rings true. But those who stay the course realize that, along the way, they've become better preachers. Frankly, those who "practice what they preach" make the best musical evangelists.

"Group singing has been scientifically proven to lower stress, relieve anxiety, and elevate endorphins."
—*Stacy Horn (2013 Time magazine article)*

High and Rough C's

"I have always believed that opera is a planet where the muses work together, join hands and celebrate all the arts."
—Franco Zeffirelli (b. 1923)

Opera is the most spectacularly striking musical art form I know. It just doesn't do much for me.

Beautifully produced and performed grand operatic productions combine fabulous singing and playing, inspired acting and staging, and stunning costumes and sets. This all works together to create an often opulent, undeniably powerful musical spectacle.

For me, though, it's overkill. Frankly, as an oratorio guy— and one who loves orchestral and choral music — I find the opera spectacle distracting and overstimulating. I'm certainly an outlier on this opinion, but I do find it a bit irritating that so many beautiful melodies are written for operas.

I would imagine that my midwestern frugal sensibilities and my easily distractible nature help shape my opinions on opera. Moliere thought, "Of all the noises known to man, opera is the most expensive."

In contrast, oratorio needs no sets, costumes, or action to make it effective.

I find that perfectly nice singers often act differently when they put on makeup and costumes — and, usually, not for the better. Even one of the world's most famous opera composers, Rossini, stated, "How wonderful opera would be if there were no singers."

Another issue I often hear with opera singers is that their voices sometimes become less controlled, with wide, unwieldy vibratos. When a voice becomes too big and wobbly, it becomes less attractive to me. I compare this type of voice to a body-builder whose muscles are so overdeveloped that they lose the beauty of human form.

I fully understand that this is most likely a minority opinion in the world of music lovers, and that millions of people view opera as their favorite musical genre. Many of these incurable opera lovers are friends of mine whose opinions I respect.

So I hope they'll respect how my experiences have informed my beliefs. My point of view has been shaped by either knowing too little or too much about it. But I do support the opera genre in our curricular offerings, because it's an important subject and art form.

The social context surrounding opera has also confounded me. It seems that the general public often goes to the opera for the purpose of being seen. Voltaire, too, was confused by this phenomenon, stating that, "The opera is nothing but a public gathering place, where we assemble on certain days without precisely knowing why."

Mark Twain said, "To me an opera is the very climax and capstone of the absurd, the fantastic, the unjustifiable. I hate the very name of opera — partly because of the nights of suffering I have endured in its presence, and partly because I want to love it and can't. I suppose one naturally hates the things he wants to love and can't. In America the opera is an affectation. The seeming love for [it] is a lie."

Having conducted and sung in a few operas, I don't find the work much different from that of conducting oratorios. It isn't a lack of familiarity with the music that causes my problem with opera. Remember, after all, I'm an oratorio guy.

"Every theatre is an insane asylum, but an opera theatre is the ward for the incurables."

—*Franz Schalk (1863-1931)*

True Test

"The true test of a man's character is what he does when no one is watching."

—John Wooden (1910-2010)

Many years ago, while I was working at my desk at Rollins College over winter break, I looked out my window and saw Fred Rogers — better known as Mister Rogers —crossing the street by Keene Music Hall.

Fred and his wife Joanne were both Rollins alumni, and would often spend a month or so in Winter Park during the winter.

Fred happened to see a piece of paper by the curb, and stopped to picked it up and deposit it in a nearby by trash container before continuing on his trek to the college swimming pool, where he exercised.

What I observed was an absolutely non-remarkable, remarkable act — but it spoke volumes about Fred's character. He had no idea that I was on the campus and looking out my office window. He picked up the trash because it was simply the right thing to do.

This kind of selfless act seems to be becoming less common, and everyone wants to get "credit" for good deeds.

Our Department of Music is blessed with colleagues who work together for the good of our students. It's rare to find a group of talented artists and educators so willing to put egos aside and work together — and when it happens, the results can be quite astonishing.

President Harry Truman said, "You can accomplish anything in life, provided that you don't mind who gets the credit."

Additionally, if "What goes around comes around," then if you do right by others, you're doing what's right for you.

"Real integrity is doing the right thing, knowing that nobody's going to know whether you did it or not."
—*Oprah Winfrey (b. 1954)*

You Can't Hide

"Music is a higher revelation than all wisdom and philosophy.

Music is the electrical soil in which the spirit lives, thinks, and invents."

-Ludwig van Beethoven (1770-1827)

Music exposes phonies.

During intermission at a piano recital, I told a colleague that while the technical ability of the artist was impressive, his playing hadn't moved me.

She agreed and added that the pianist's "spirit" was wrong. This prompted me to listen differently after intermission, and her opinion was validated.

When an artist is in command of his or her craft, personality should come through. The listener should hear the artist's spirit.

Special training isn't required to hear music-making at this level. Famed composer Aaron Copland wrote about listening to music at various "planes," and described them as follows:

1. *The Sensual Plane* is where you hear music, but not closely enough to develop an opinion about it. In essence, it's background music.

2. *The Expressive Plane* is where you hear music, and note how it makes you feel or what it might represent.

3. *The Sheerly Musical Plane* is listening to the elements of music, such as tempo, pitch, harmonic structure, dynamics, and so forth.

Try listening to music at all three levels, and see if the music becomes more vivid. Perhaps those with a fair amount of musical training might actually be at a disadvantage.

Why do I say that?

Knowledge about what it takes for a performer to achieve a demonstrated level of technical prowess means practicing deeper listening. But it could also mean it is a distraction from expressive listening.

When a performer has mastered a work thoroughly, and can bring his or her personal expressivity to the performance, it becomes art — and the performer is a "musician's musician". A rare accolade, indeed.

This is also the case for composers. What a composer writes allows listeners to see the person — for better or worse — behind the music. It's difficult for them to hide.

Richard Wagner is a prime example. He was a scoundrel. He was anti-Semitic, a womanizer, and he belonged to questionable political parties.

Wagner was hugely arrogant and self-serving, and was known not to honor his financial obligations. Even the philosopher Nietzsche asked, "Is Wagner a human being at all? Is he not rather a disease?"

There is no question, Wagner wrote some fabulous music. But because of the reasons I mentioned, I have a difficult time programming his music. I believe that I hear the person in his compositions.

The opposite effect also occurs. While I'm conducting, I also experience the spirit of composers. For example, I hear and sense the gentle soul of Mendelssohn, the fun-loving spirit of Mozart, the religious devotion of Bach, the warm heart of Dvorak, and the tortured soul of Beethoven.

These great musicians, and countless others, don't want or need to hide. The more of their respective lives you know, the more you understand and can relate to their humanity — and the circumstances that shaped their music.

As unique, and even peculiar, as many master musicians are, they want you to experience their art. They want to share their heart with you. This is true soul music.

"What is uttered from the heart alone, will win the hearts of others to your own."
   —Johann von Goethe (1749-1832)

Lead Like You Have Lived

"How far you go in life depends on you being tender with the young, compassionate with the aged, sympathetic with the striving, and tolerant of the weak and the strong. Because sometime in life you will be all of these."
—*George Washington Carver (1861-1943)*

I keep that quote by George Washington Carver under the glass top on my desk. It reminds me that as a teacher and an administrator, I must understand all of the various stages in a person's life. It also reminds me that I have been "all of these" at one time or another.

I'm pretty sure I thought I was hell on wheels as a young man. Not to worry, though. Life has a way of making us all feel mortal.

While I don't believe I was ever mean, rude, or disrespectful, I was ambitious and self-assured — whether justified or not. Sometimes I wondered if my ambition was driven by my thirst for success, or by my fear of failure.

Every year I teach, I learn something new. Teachers of merit are lifelong learners. To make this tangible in my life, I keep a jar of leaves and a basket full of rocks in my office. Every year, I put a few leaves in the jar and I recite the first stanza of the poem "A Leaf Treader" by Robert Frost:

I have been treading on leaves all day until I am autumn-tired.

God knows all the color and forms of leaves I have trodden on and mired.

Perhaps I have put forth too much strength and been too fierce from fear.

I have safely trodden under foot the leaves of another year.

This poem continues to speak to me, as does the symbolism I place on the basket of rocks. The hundreds of rocks are from all over the world. They remind me of where I've been — but more importantly, of who I am.

They remind me of how I'm a mere blink in history, and that humans have always had a love and need for the physical world in which we live. My rocks are from Walden Pond, the stream on my family's farm, the Appian Way, Lake Tahoe, Troy, Key West, the Berlin Wall, Florence, Monticello, the Grand Canyon, and so forth. You get the idea.

They're from where people — some famous, some not — lived their respective lives. And for a brief time, I share that life's journey with those who have gone before.

Many years ago, an annoyed senior music major came to my office after a rehearsal. He complained that our new freshman bassist was a "know it all" and asked me to "put him in his place."

I explained that every year or so there's a student who has yet to learn the art of humility and respect for protocol. I went on to say that one of the most "self-assured" students I ever taught was a freshman just three years ago.

My student asked, "How did he turn out?" I responded, "I think quite well. How do you think you're doing?" After an awkward pause, he asked, "Was I really like that?"

I responded, "Yes, but you're worth the investment, and so is the freshman you're referencing." A perfect example of how time brings perspective. I wouldn't have been as tolerant in my earlier years as a teacher.

Aristotle said it best: "The roots of education are bitter, but the fruit is sweet." Teaching is a noble profession, and it takes knowledge of your subject matter and love for sharing it to be effective.

A master teacher does much more than guiding his or her students on how to discover their respective talents while they are accumulating knowledge. A master teacher is a purveyor of transformative education — which can only happen when one is tolerant, tough, and tender, all at the same time.

"Teaching music is not my main purpose. I want to make good citizens. If a child hears fine music from the day of his birth, and learns to play it himself, he develops sensitivity, discipline, and endurance. He gets a beautiful heart."
—Shinichi Suzuki (1898-1998)

EPILOGUE

That's Not What I Heard

Therefore, in order to keep me from becoming conceited, I was given a thorn in my flesh, a messenger of Satan, to torment me. Three times I pleaded with the Lord to take it away from me. But he said to me, "My grace is sufficient for you, for my power is made perfect in weakness." Therefore I will boast all the more gladly about my weaknesses, so that Christ's power may rest on me. That is why, for Christ's sake, I delight in weaknesses, in insults, in hardships, in persecutions, in difficulties. For when I am weak, then I am strong.

—*2 Corinthians 12:7-10*

It takes more than a lifetime to fully understand oneself. I always knew that I processed sounds differently. In my youth I remember thinking, "That's not what I heard."

My mother, who was an educator, recognized that I didn't learn like others. Because of her perceptiveness, she would not allow schools to administer standardized tests to me until my college-board exams.

When I was in the 6th grade, I overheard her arguing with my principal, telling him, "John is plenty smart, but he doesn't think like everyone else, and doing poorly on tests could make him think he's not smart and could hurt his future." Over and over I heard her say, "I don't want him labeled."

Learning disabilities aren't new. The early Egyptians and Greeks wrote about them. When I was in elementary school, there was no established method of dealing with children who learned differently. There wasn't a federal law mandating support for children with learning disabilities until I was in high school.

I'd been compensating my whole life. What else could I have done? During dictation exercises in college Music Theory class, I came to grips with the fact that sometimes I'd hear sounds backwards, or jumbled.

Even then, fearing embarrassment, I just figured it out. Fast forward to my doctorate, and its foreign language requirement. I had asked a colleague to help me study. After watching me struggle, he speculated about the reason for my difficulty. He also suggested someone who could — and did — confirm that I had a recognized condition.

It's called auditory processing disorder (APD), which is a catchall term for a multitude of disorders that affect the way the brain processes auditory information. I refer to my problem as auditory dyslexia.

The first research on APD actually started the year I was born. But it wasn't until the late '70s that specialists met to discuss the disorder. By then, I was in the classroom teaching.

How do I cope? My brain "auto corrects" sounds. I imagine it's like someone who's bilingual, but whose first language isn't English. When spoken to in English, that person automatically translates the words into his or her first language.

If I'm tired or not feeling my best, it requires more effort to keep sounds straight. Working in a noisy environment or communicating while others are speaking is a challenge — and singing in foreign languages can be a tough task.

My son Taylor was around 7 years old when he strode up to Fred Rogers, the leading citizen of Mr. Rogers' Neighborhood, and struck a Power Ranger pose. Typical of Fred, his response was simultaneously simple and profound. He pointed to Taylor's chest and said, "You know, the power is really inside of you."

Why did I select music as a career? I think the challenge of it selected me. Music was inside of me; I just needed to decipher the puzzle. (Actually I really wanted to be a baseball player, but one thing got in the way: Not enough skill.)

This line from Harper Lee's *To Kill a Mockingbird*, as spoken by Atticus Finch, resonated with me: "You never really know a man until you understand things from his point of view, until you climb into his skin and walk around in it."

In Malcolm Gladwell's *David and Goliath*, he explores the role of learning disabilities in making the person. He points out that many people with learning disabilities have been quite successful, and wonders if "because of their disorder … they learned something in their struggle that proved to be of enormous advantage."

I'm lucky to have learned how to manage my ability, not to dwell on my disability. In many ways, APD has made me listen more carefully, and assisted me in developing skills others don't seem to possess.

I'm convinced that most people have some sort of learning disability. And those who learn to hide the wheels on their proverbial wheelchair are stronger for the challenge.

"My advice to other disabled people would be, concentrate on things your disability doesn't prevent you doing well, and don't regret the things it interferes with. Don't be disabled in spirit as well as physically."
—Stephen Hawking (b. 1942)

ABOUT JOHN V. SINCLAIR

For more than three decades, John V. Sinclair has shared his talent and dedication to musical excellence. Dr. Sinclair enjoys a national reputation as a conductor of choral masterworks. Now in his 28th season as Artistic Director and Conductor of the Bach Festival Society, he continues his imaginative programming, creative interpretations, and expressive conducting style.

Dr. Sinclair has made hundreds of appearances as conductor, clinician, or lecturer throughout the United States and the world. The Bach Festival, under his leadership, has achieved international recognition by touring in Europe, producing nationally released CDs, and performing with the London Symphony during their Florida residencies.

As a conductor, he is equally adept at directing choral and orchestral music. In addition to Rollins College and the Bach Festival, he is conductor of the International Moravian Music Festivals in North Carolina and Pennsylvania, and Orlando's Messiah Choral Society. He has led over 800 performances of Epcot's Candlelight Processional, and is a frequent conductor for the Berkshire Choral International Festivals and Orlando Ballet.

Considered a master teacher, Dr. Sinclair is Director of Music and holds the John M. Tiedtke Endowed Chair at Rollins College. Among his many awards are the Sidney Algernon Sullivan Citizen Award, the Arthur Vining Davis Fellowship, the Barden and McKean Teaching Awards, the Cornell Distinguished Service Award, and the "Outstanding Music Educator of the Year" by United Arts of Central Florida.

Dr. Sinclair holds Masters and Doctoral degrees from the University of Missouri-Kansas City's Conservatory of Music. His undergraduate school, William Jewell College, honored him in 2013 with its prestigious Citation for Achievement.

For more information, visit www.JohnVSinclair.com

ACKNOWLEDGMENTS

To my son Taylor, daughter Kaley, and son-in-law Vish, who have long-suffered a busy, story-telling father.

With grateful appreciation to Jeanne Marie Antoinette and Paul Peterson of Phenomenal Publishing for their publishing expertise and guidance in creating this book, including Jeanne Marie's artwork and layout talent, and Paul's keen editing eye.

The author gratefully acknowledges the reading and suggestions made in the writing of this book by Randy Noles and Dr. James Armstrong.

To my talented and kindhearted colleagues (past and present) in the Rollins College Department of Music whose collegiality has made showing up to work rewarding and, most days, enjoyable: Chuck Archard, Dr. Gloria Cook, Dr. Daniel Crozier, Daniel Flick, Dr. William Gallo, Dr. John Grau, Dr. Susan Lackman, Dr. Edmund LeRoy, Dr. Caitlin Mohr, Sherry Orr, Jamey Ray, Joni Roos, Susan Throm-White, and Dr. Sunni Witmer.

As all career educators know, the best way to keep learning is to teach. I am grateful to the thousands of students who have taught me so much.

To members of the Bach Festival Choir and Orchestra who inspire me each and every time we make music. Their love and dedication to music, combined with their individual and collective musicianship, are an affirmation to the power of music.

To the Bach Festival's Society's two long-term presidents who have been wise mentors, and who have demonstrated a selfless dedication to our community that has perpetuated this wonderful organization: John Tiedtke and Eric Ravndal, III.

Also a deep appreciation for the other presidents with whom I have served: Michael Murphy, Philip Tiedtke, and Autumn Ames. And thank you for the support of the Trustees and colleagues who comprise the Society's Artistic Committee: Beverly Slaughter and Michael Kakos, Dr. Gloria Cook, and Rhonda Burnham, artistic and educational manager. And a heartfelt thank you to all current and past Bach Festival Board of Trustees members; Elizabeth Gwinn, executive director, and Stephanie Rivera, communication manager.

To Dr. Nola Reed Knouse, Executive Director of the Moravian Music Foundation, and all my Moravian friends. Your commitment to the music that reveals your faith has heightened mine.

To the senior ministers of First Congregational Church with whom I have served: Dr. William Tuck, Dr. James Armstrong, Bryan Fulwider and Shawn Garvey. To my colleagues: Chris Olivent and Walter Kimble, and all who make music and make it possible.

To Music Directors Rick Mizell and Ted Ricketts and all the Cast Members at Walt Disney World for helping to make Magic each show.

To the leadership and membership of the Messiah Choral Society.

To Dr. Michael Barimo, Dr. Paul Dreyer, Dr. Thomas Hand, Dr. Victor McNamara, Dr. Jason Nitzsche, Dr. Victor Roberts, Dr. David Vaughan, Jr., and Dr. George White, whose knowledge and skill make it possible for me to continue my craft.

And finally, to all those whose attendance and patronage have sparked the passion and the means to continue to make music.

Book cover and design by Jeanne Marie Antoinette.
Front cover photograph by Rafael Tongol.